# INDESTRUCTIBLE

*Praises for*
# INDESTRUCTIBLE

Honest, vulnerable, and a thoughtful narrator, Ally shows us through storytelling how hard and beautiful it is to be human. She bares her soul to her readers and cracks the healing process wide open, never claiming to be high or mighty but unafraid to be raw. This is a book that will leave you highlighting the pages and going back to reread different parts. This is Ally at her best.

—**Hannah Brencher**, TED speaker, author of
*If You Find This Letter* and founder of More Love Letters

I once heard that if you ever lose love, don't go out looking for it. But, reach inside you and recreate what you think you lost because you are love. And, you can't lose you. I really didn't know what that meant or the depths of brokenness that it would take me until after I was cut from my 3rd NFL team and walked away from the only thing I've known and truly loved in my life. Feeling lost, vulnerable and drowning in what seemed to be a sea of shame and self-hatred, I would have given anything to pick up this book during that season. Not only will it serve as a compass pointing you back home, but it is also a prophetic voice that will lead you into the beautiful, messy process of owning your story and help you realize that you aren't a summary of all the nights that broke you.

Without a doubt, I feel like a new person after reading this book.

—**Caleb Campbell**, NFL Draft Pick,
Former Army Officer, West Point, Public Speaker

Ally brilliantly and accurately captures the experience of what it looks like to recover from a traumatic experience and take ownership of your future. Anyone who has suffered because of their choices or because of the choices of someone they love will resonate with her story and follow with her on her brave journey to freedom.

—**Austin Eubanks**, TEDx Speaker, COO of
Foundry Treatment Center

We stand anew in a bright world where women have the courage to speak up about mistreatment and abuse running. Ally Fallon's voice is a leading one in this movement. I'm confident this book will give you the courage to find your way to the truth and to freedom as safely, as she did.

—**Claire Diaz-Ortiz**, bestselling author,
speaker and early employee of Twitter

Everyone knows pain, this is a universal fact. In Ally's heartbreakingly beautiful book Indestructible, she shares what its like to have the dreams of your youth shattered from emotional abuse, divorce, and loss to then realizing that embracing her pain and changing the narrative of her story to one where she is her own hero. *Indestructible* teaches us what it practically looks like to start the life long process of loving and healing ourselves by owning and facing the darkest parts of our stories.

—**Ruthie Lindsey**, Public Speaker, Author and Podcast Host

Ally's story is not just one of heartbreak; it's a story of healing, resilience and strength. A true fighter, who has opened her heart and story to help heal yours too. A real page-turner, and a book I finished in a day.

—**Lindsey Caldwell**, Reporter/Host, Work has been
on E! News, Entertainment Tonight, and TIME

*Indestructible* is beautifully-told love story and shows a clear pathway for any woman looking to begin again. Ally shows us how truth and expression will always lead us to exactly where we're meant to be.

You'll be reminded and encouraged through the vulnerability of her experiences that the greatest journey we take onward is actually the return to ourselves. This is the perfect read for any woman who has ever lost herself in the pursuit of love.

—**Maxie McCoy**, author of *You're Not Lost*,
Host and Executive Producer of *Let Her Speak*

Ally's story is a remarkable testament to the strength of a young woman determined to stand in truth and wholeness. Watching Ally take off the blinders and face the reality of the pain she had been living under in a broken marriage—and begin untie the invisible emotional and mental knots that years of abuse binds—we see a woman slowly come alive again in wholeness: mind, body, spirit. Ally reminds us once again that the only way to deal with the pain is to walk directly through the fire, not around. Her story of facing the pain, is one that will resonate with any woman, any human, who is running after a life grounded in truth and humility, and fueled by courage. Walking alongside and bearing witness to her coming alive again and back home to herself has been a great privilege. I am proud of beautiful gift with words that Ally possesses, but more so than that—I am proud of my friend.

—**Beth Murray**, The Family Institute at Northwestern,
former Network Producer NBC's TODAY Show.

How desperately we need women willing to show us the way to discover and live our true selves! In *Indestructible*, Ally does exactly this. Rather than tidy "lessons learned," this book is uncomfortably full of unfolding growth (outside our comfort zone is the only place we authentically grow, by the way). There are no abstract platitudes within these pages; she leads by example. All of this transformational possibility AND it is served within some of the most skillful writing I've ever read. I can't recommend the stories and truths, life and wisdom of Ally Fallon and *Indestructible* enough.

—**Lisa Whelchel**, Actress, Author,
Speaker and CoActive Life Coach

As a woman working in the entertainment industry, I know how important it is for women to speak up about the abuse and mistreatment they have suffered. Each time one woman shares her story, you know it's representative of many other stories, and we all gain the courage to speak our truth and create an environment of safety and trust. I'm grateful to Ally for her courage in going first. I know she'll inspire you to because she inspires me.

—**Amy Brown**, @radioamy, Co-Host of
the Nationally Syndicated Bobby Bones Show

# INDESTRUCTIBLE

## LEVERAGING YOUR
## BROKEN HEART
## TO BECOME A FORCE
## OF LOVE & CHANGE
## IN THE WORLD

### ALLISON FALLON

NEW YORK

LONDON • NASHVILLE • MELBOURNE • VANCOUVER

# INDESTRUCTIBLE
## LEVERAGING YOUR BROKEN HEART TO BECOME A FORCE OF LOVE & CHANGE IN THE WORLD

© 2019 **ALLISON FALLON**

Published in New York, New York, by Morgan James Publishing. Morgan James is a trademark of Morgan James, LLC. www.MorganJamesPublishing.com

The Morgan James Speakers Group can bring authors to your live event. For more information or to book an event visit The Morgan James Speakers Group at www.TheMorganJamesSpeakersGroup.com.

ISBN 978-1-68350-975-2  paperback
ISBN 978-1-68350-976-9  eBook
Library of Congress Control Number: 2018934763

In an effort to support local communities, raise awareness and funds, Morgan James Publishing donates a percentage of all book sales for the life of each book to Habitat for Humanity Peninsula and Greater Williamsburg.

Get involved today! Visit
www.MorganJamesBuilds.com

"I believe a strong woman may be stronger than a man, particularly if she happens to have love in her heart. I guess a loving woman is *indestructible*."
—**John Steinbeck**, East of Eden

# TABLE OF CONTENTS

*To me—the love of my own life—and to anyone else who has had to fight like hell to save her own soul.*

*We are spectacular.*

# ACKNOWLEDGEMENTS

Every book ever written is a team effort, and this one is no exception.

I'd like to to thank my friends Betsy and Katie, for being the a safe harbor when I needed it most. Without you, this would not be my life, let alone my book.

Beth, for all of the hours you spent on the phone with me, and in person, reminding me I wasn't crazy. And for the magic blanket. And The Peacemaker.

Steve and Gracie, Jill and Kate. For letting me crash in your guest rooms when I couldn't go home, and for all the advice and wine. I loved being your roommates.

Kelly & CJ & Selah—for all those times you texted to say, "here's what's for dinner… come on over."

Annalea. For being my fighter friend. For teaching me how good it feels to say the f word. And for being protective of me when I couldn't be protective of myself.

The women from the Holy Land. The longest text thread in the history of text threads. Thanks for being the kind of women I'm writing this book about. I learn so much from you.

Vanessa. For all the times you've listened and let me scream and cry. And for letting me raid your closet.

To my "Book Club" ladies. Mary, Tracie, Lindsley, Emily, Madeleine... for teaching me about Jade Eggs over champagne in the morning. You keep me interesting.

Ashley and Bryan. For being the kind of Christians who actually love people like Jesus did.

To my family. Mom and Dad, Mandee and Ryan, Braden and Rachel. Rilo and Levi. For your decades of consistent love and support. I want to be more like all of you when I grow up.

To my editors, Beks and Cadence. Thanks for making me look like a better writer than I am.

To David. I will never forget your kindness.

And to you, dear reader, wherever you are. Somehow, without even knowing you, I love you. You are indestructible.

# INTRODUCTION
# ON BECOMING INDESTRUCTIBLE

*"When the worst thing that has ever happened to you happens, you will realize you don't have any reason to be afraid anymore"*
**—Robi Damelin**

You are remarkable—there are very few things I know to be true in this life, but this is one of them. You have so much beauty, so much passion, so much love and life to bring to this world. We *need* you. I know life tempts you, at times, to numb yourself, hide yourself, injure yourself, dumb yourself down, even to give up on yourself all together. Please, please don't do that. We are dying for everything you have to give us—in all its flaming glory.

I say this to you now, after everything that has happened, but I never used to think this could be true about me. Other people, maybe, but not me. That is until my life exploded and everything fell apart.

It was a fall night, and I went over to a friend's house for a formal showing of a documentary. The video was about The Israeli and Palestinian Conflict, and to be honest, this was the last thing on my mind. Who even knows why I pulled myself together to go that night. Maybe it was to get out of the house, which was feeling dark and stale and unbearable during this time. Regardless, there I was, perched on a stool behind a couch.

After the film, a woman named Robi got up and told her story about how her son had been killed in the conflict.

Robi was beautiful. That's what I thought as she stood there speaking to us. She was about 5 feet 6 inches, heavyset, and wrapped in a multi-colored dress. Her accent was soft, like half-melted butter. Her hair was cut quite close to her head, and her skin was golden and glowing.

She seemed so much stronger than me. That's what I remember thinking. Grounded. Fearless. A force to be reckoned with.

Her son, a Jewish soldier, had been killed by a Palestinian sniper. She shared how this experience had broken her heart, broken her *open*, and eventually launched her into the peace work she's doing now in one of the most conflict-ridden parts of the world.

She talked about hatred and greed and grief and control and power, and how the only way to heal the world was by learning to love the people we think we hate. The ones we don't understand. The ones who have hurt us, betrayed us, broken us, lied to us, lied about us, attacked us. The ones who have left us lost, confused, and abandoned.

As she spoke, I have to admit, I hated the way I felt. My husband JD sat next to me. I stared forward.

This was back in 2013, by the way, which for me at least, was a time when the hatred and violence in our world felt much easier to ignore. It was a far away, "out there", under-the-surface kind of problem—a dull, fuzzy, volume-down-low kind of thing. It's easy for us to ignore evil when it's not hurting us in a personal way, especially when we are armored up or have hardened ourselves against feeling it. As I listened, I thought about how glad I was to live in a part of the world where violence like this wasn't my everyday reality.

This, again, was before an American gunman set up shop in a hotel window and opened fire at a country music festival in Las Vegas, killing 58 innocent people and injuring nearly 500. It was before a Texas man walked into a church with an assault rifle, mercilessly killing 26 innocent attendees—women and children included. It was before a violent and angry protestor at a "Unite the Right" rally in Charlottesville rammed his car into an unsuspecting crowd. Before a deranged gunman claimed 49 lives in a nightclub in Orlando. It's amazing how much we tend to endure before we wake up and pay attention.

This was also before I had admitted to anyone the truth of my marriage.

At this point, JD and I had been married for almost three years. We had a whirlwind romance story—the kind you'd repeat at parties and that would make everyone lean in and smile and shake their heads in disbelief.

When our romance unfolded, I was a new author, working on my first book and writing for various publications online. JD stumbled across an article I'd written. When he read my story, he thought to himself, *I have to meet that girl.* Or, at least, that's how he would tell the story. A few short months after meeting, we were married.

JD was a pastor at a church, and so by default, I became a pastor's wife. This was ok with me at the time—maybe even more than ok—since I had also grown up in church and had always said I wanted to marry a man of faith. The fact that he was a pastor seemed like an upgrade to that request. The only problem—and this was a big problem—was marriage turned out to be quite different than I expected.

In the early days, members of our church, who knew I was a newlywed, would pull me aside and say things like, "isn't being married just the *best*? Isn't it like a constant sleepover with your best friend?" They would have the most sincere looks on their faces when they said these things, so I would smile and nod and laugh along with them, then walk away feeling like I was suffocating.

For me, if I was being honest, marriage felt like prison. Not that I had ever been in prison before, but if I had to imagine being in prison, this is what I guessed it would feel like. Dark and lonely. A general sense of dread, as if something terrible was always about to happen. Rarely a space or a place where I could let my guard down. At one point, I remember wondering how long it had been since I *hadn't* woken up in the morning in a panic.

We fought. All the time. It would start over the smallest thing—how I was loading the dishwasher incorrectly, or a bill that had been misplaced or not been paid on time. One time, he became furious with me for "lying" to him about how many tortillas were left in the refrigerator. I told him there were two, when there were actually three or four. That fight escalated and ended, as so many of our arguments did, with me running from the house without any shoes on. I had tried everything I knew to stop the fighting. Nothing was working.

I suggested we go to counseling, but this did not seem like an option to JD. My dad is a psychologist, and has been working with married couples for more than 30 years, so I would sometimes casually mention how my dad says counseling is for every marriage, not just a marriage in crisis. One day JD became so infuriated by my repeated hinting that he assured me if I brought it up again, he'd make sure it was the last time. So I stopped asking.

To top it all off, I made my living as a writer, but now every time I sat down at my computer, I felt stuck. All locked up. No matter how hard I tried, I couldn't get the words to flow again. I was trying to write a book about marriage. Our marriage, I guess. About the challenges and rewards, about how selfless love was our only chance for foraging a new way forward. But the longer I worked at this, the more I started to wonder if I even believed myself. Love had failed me—or perhaps it was that I had failed at love.

The strangest part of all of this is that when Robi started talking about hate that night, it wasn't him—JD—who came to my mind. It was me. *What a joke of a woman I was,* I told myself, *that at 30 years old, I still couldn't manage to be in an adult relationship.* I was actually furious at myself for not being able to hold my own in an argument, livid about how quickly I would lose track of myself—of what I wanted or needed or was trying to say.

How pathetic must I be that even after giving JD everything he'd asked for, everything he'd wanted, even the things I hadn't wanted to give, I still couldn't make him happy. I couldn't make the fighting stop. How could I be a force of love and change in the world when I couldn't even be a force of love and change in my own marriage?

Meanwhile, Robi was standing there strong and beautiful, talking about making peace with our enemies. Real enemies. A man who had murdered her son. I had an *easy* life, really—a beautiful new home, a nice car, food on my table. A husband who took care of me. I was just being a drama queen. What was wrong with me?

Robi introduced her friend Basham, a Palestinian man who had also lost a child in the conflict—his daughter. She was killed by an Israeli soldier outside of her school one morning.

As Basham spoke, I suddenly remembered how months earlier I had been convinced I was pregnant with a baby girl. It was too soon to tell, but I was sure. Just so sure. That is, until I sat on the toilet watching the water turn red and swirling and screaming to myself on the inside, wishing there were something I could do to stop it.

It was strange for me to want to be pregnant, especially with a little girl, since my home didn't even feel like a safe place for *me* to be, let alone a baby. But some part of me thought having a baby might fix everything.

For some odd reason, I thought that if anyone could bring peace to this situation, *she* could. I cried for days over that loss—a "daughter" who was not even a daughter, the death of someone I hadn't even met.

Basham talked about his friendship with Robi, and about The Parents Circle Families Forum (PCFF), which is a large group of parents and family members who gather together regularly from both sides of the conflict to talk about love and loss, and how they might find a way to peace. They meet in Bethlehem, one of the only places in the Holy Land where both Israelis and Palestinians can gather together. "We refuse to be enemies," Basham said. That is their motto.

I didn't like it. I thought about what it would mean for me to *refuse* to be enemies with JD. If this was the way forward in love—and I worried it was—what was I supposed to do? If there was more I needed to do, where on earth was I going to find the courage and strength to do it? Everything I had to give, I had given. How much could one person be expected to endure?

After we were done that night with the documentary, I waited to introduce myself to Robi. I wanted to meet her. I felt like she might be able to help. I tiptoed in her direction, aware of JD's eyes on me, and rehearsed what I might say. Something clever. Something intelligent. Something memorable. But by the time the crowd of people around her had dispersed and I was looking at her face, all of the words I'd rehearsed were gone.

I stuttered and tripped over a few phrases, before I finally managed to say four words.

"You are so brave."

She leaned in really closely and put her hand on my arm. She looked at me warmly, like we were friends. I will never forget that look. When she spoke, it was barely above a whisper. She said, "When the worst thing that has ever happened to you *happens*, you will realize you don't have any reason to be afraid anymore."

I nodded. It would be another eighteen months before I understood exactly what she meant.

# CHAPTER 1
# TELL ME THE TRUTH

*"Tell me every terrible thing you ever did,*
*and let me love you anyway."*
—**Sade Andria Zabala**, Coffee and Cigarettes

The first thing I noticed when I started going to yoga at a studio was the way our breathing sounded when we all did it together. It was September, so just starting to get cold outside, but not the terrible bone-chilling kind of cold—the kind that still has a little warmth left to it, sort of gentle and romantic. We would all huddle together in that yoga room on chilly mornings and brisk afternoons and just *breathe* together. In and out. In and out. Like the ocean.

I remember realizing for the first time that day how shallow my breath had been for so long. I wondered when the last time was that I had really taken a breath all the way in, and then all the way out again—the way they coached us to do. It was so simple, so impossibly simple. And yet somehow I had been missing it.

One of the first people I met at the studio was Sarah, an instructor who I noticed right away because of her flaming red hair and shining smile. She had this way of looking people right in the eyes when she was talking to them—like she *really saw them*, you know? That's what I thought when I met Sarah.

I also thought she seemed happy. Stupidly happy, actually. Sometimes out of nowhere she would throw her arms up in the air and let out this uncontrollable squeal—the sound of an elementary school kid being let out to recess. Part of me wondered if she must be on drugs or something.

And still, many times after class, this strange urge would come over me to pull Sarah aside and tell her everything. What had happened to me. What he had done. Why I had let him. Telling her made no sense, but I was desperate, and sometimes when we are desperate, we do things that make no sense.

So one day, after class, we were bumping around in that small lobby outside of the studio, and I blurted something out. Of all the things I could have blurted out, this was the strangest one, but it was the only thing I could think of at the time—the only way I could fathom to get things moving.

During a lull in conversation, I opened my mouth and said that JD and I were trying to get pregnant. We'd been trying for nearly two years now. Trying to Conceive. *TTC*. That's what they called it in all of those ridiculous online forums I found myself compulsively reading late at night. I asked Sarah if she thought yoga might help.

She leaned in.

I wasn't expecting this. We didn't know each other. We had exchanged names. But other than that, she had no idea who I was.

She told me that if I felt comfortable, I could take my right hand and put it on my belly—really low, yes, right there, over my reproductive organs. I thought it was strange that she would ask me to do that, since I was telling her something might be wrong with my reproductive organs. Still, I complied, mostly because I felt like I owed her at this point. Then she said if it felt ok, I could take my left hand and put it over my heart—yes, just like that, so I could feel it beating in my chest.

I stood there, both of my hands on my body, looking at her, waiting for something to happen. Sarah looked at me, wide-eyed, as if I should understand what she meant.

I did not understand what she meant. In fact, I just kept standing there, hands touching my belly and my heart, thinking about how strange it was that I didn't feel any connection to myself. I felt all frozen. Locked up. Almost like I didn't exist.

"I can't promise you yoga will get you a baby," Sarah said, reaching over and squeezing my arm. "But it will get you *you*—and, well… you'll see. Just keep showing up." She smiled that big Sarah smile of hers and, without any further explanation, walked away.

———————

In order for you to follow what I'm about to tell you, you need to know there are three big moments around which this story hinges. For the sake of simplicity, let's call these moments *episode one, episode two,* and *episode three.* They are spread out over the course of four years, and each one is progressively more devastating than the one before it.

This is one thing I've learned since that day I met Robi, by the way—that sometimes you *think* something is worst case scenario, when you are actually only getting started.

Shortly after I met Robi, it was *episode one.* Then, six weeks after that, *episode two.* Then I started going to go to yoga. Then, another few weeks later, *episode three.*

So it was just a few weeks after that moment standing there with Sarah that everything fell apart, all the tiny pieces I had been desperately trying to hold together.

At first this seemed like the downright opposite of what Sarah had promised. But this is something else I'm learning. When it comes to life and peace and love and getting what we want, first it is painful and horrifying, and in moments, it feels like the whole world is falling apart. Then slowly, over time, we keep showing up and breathing together and eventually we *do* get it. All of it. Everything we ever wanted. It's a miracle, really. Simple. Impossibly simple.

Why are most of us missing it?

---

From the first day JD and I met to the day we got married was four months and one day. People ask me now why we had to get married so quickly, and the truth is I'm not sure. I suppose part of it was the distance between Portland, Oregon and South Florida—where I was living at the time and where JD had accepted a job at a new church. Part of it was that we were "saving ourselves" for marriage, and in our late 20's—we were tired of waiting. But looking back, I have to wonder if the biggest reason we moved so fast was because we knew deep down that if we waited, it would never work.

When I think back to my wedding day, I think mostly about how perfect it should have been—a cold but glowing day in Portland, Oregon. New Year's Eve. We found an empty warehouse building on Tenth and Everett, in the Pearl District, with exposed brick and low-hanging beams and concrete floors. It wasn't your typical wedding venue, which was exactly what I loved about it. That, and the price was right, and it was available on short notice. Two months. That's how long I had to plan the wedding.

We bought hundreds of candles from Ikea, and my friend Brittany—who offered to be our wedding planner—formed an aisle with them, running right down the center of the room. She rented chairs and filled the ceremony room, and hung pipe and drape to divide the space in half, so we could have a separate area for the reception.

I had my heart set on an archway made of willow branches and twinkle lights at the altar. But it turns out ordering willow branches from a florist in December is close to impossible on a tight budget, so my dad drove to a friend's house and—with their permission—cut down the willow tree in their backyard. He recruited my cousin, brother, and a few family friends to help him assemble the thing into the most beautiful archway, at the altar, wrapped in lights.

I'll never forget coming home from a series of errands one day, only to find that willow tree—practically the entire thing—roped securely to the top of my dad's Toyota 4runner. Both hands came up to cover my mouth, and I shook my head, thinking about how loved you can be without even knowing it.

The morning of my wedding, JD snuck into my parents' house, where I was staying for the last days before the wedding, to steal me away for a morning coffee date. He said he knew the bride and groom weren't supposed to see each other on their wedding day, but whispered that he didn't believe in that stuff anyway and just couldn't wait. We drove to my favorite coffee shop and ordered lattes and talked about how *ready* we were to be married.

But the truth, since we're telling it, was that I was not ready. I didn't want to say it—hadn't wanted to say it for weeks now—that this was all moving too fast for me, and I was feeling unsteady. I wanted to be ready. I wanted to love him the way he seemed to love me. I didn't want to be the one to shatter this idyllic story of ours. But no matter how hard I tried to get there, I couldn't do it.

Sitting at the table, JD smiled and handed me a card and gift.

"This is the first of many," he told me, smiling. "I have one for every day this week." That was JD. Smart and charming and strong and powerful, and always one step ahead of me.

"I love you so much," he said.

But as I sat there across from JD opening the gift and reading the card, I didn't feel like I imagined I would on my wedding day. I didn't *feel* like he loved me. I didn't feel happy. What was wrong with me? Here I was, sitting in front of this man who wanted to make me his wife, and I couldn't make myself fall in love with him.

---

In the weeks leading up to our wedding, I packed my things into three boxes to be shipped across the country. Immediately after the wedding, we would leave Portland—which had been home to me for most of my childhood and adult life. I would then move to an apartment JD had secured for us in West Palm Beach, Florida near the church.

JD insisted I didn't really need more than a few boxes. I wasn't going to need much. He would take care of everything. And besides, he wanted us to start fresh together. It was better for us not to get too sentimental about things, he said. Not to let our past keep us from our future. That sounded like a nice idea to me, so I went with it. I sifted through my things, one by one.

There was a headlamp I'd bought from a store called Next Adventure when my best friend Mikey and I went to Peru to hike Machu Picchu. A copy of *The Artist's Way* my friend Noah had given to me while we worked together at a restaurant in the Pearl District. The dented U-lock I had used to lock up my bike all over the city. For years that bike had been my only form of transportation.

I held that heavy metal lock in my hands and remembered the hundreds of times I had biked to meet friends for brunch on a Saturday morning—how we would eat and then ride for hours, up to Mt. Tabor or down to Powell's Books.

I stared at an old pair of running shoes and remembered all the times I had circled the waterfront loop with my friend Rebecca. I thought about the feeling of crossing the finish line at the Portland Marathon this past fall. It was a thousand times harder than I imagined, but I had done it.

There was an old, tattered book of Billy Collins' poetry, *Sailing Alone Around the Room*. Which obviously made me think of all the walks with my friend Noah in the Pearl District, reading and memorizing those sweet, simple, perfect lines.

I picked up a dingy pillow. It had been white at some point and had a giant sunflower on it. It was ugly, actually, now that I was looking at it. But it made me think of that tiny little apartment I'd lived in on the corner of NW 21st and Flanders, with two of my best friends, and how many people we'd crammed into our living room to watch episodes of *Lost*, or the 2008 Presidential debates and election.

I thought of all the times we'd walked down the street to the Blue Moon Diner, to eat spicy tater tots at 11pm on a work night because one of us couldn't sleep, or because some guy had broken up with one of us over text message. I held the pillow to my face, remembering. It smelled kind of musty.

"Please don't make a big deal about the pillows," JD said, coming through the doorway. "I'll buy you new ones when we get to Florida. Any pillows you want."

I looked up, startled.

"Oh, sorry," I said, embarrassed to have been caught in that memory. JD moved into the room.

"Don't make this a sad thing," he said, sitting down next to me on the bed and putting his hand on my leg. "It's not sad. You're letting go of some things, but you're getting a *husband*."

He smiled.

I looked at my feet and forced a smile, too. I knew when he said that, he wasn't talking about the pillow. He was talking about Mikey. I shoved the sunflower pillow into the trash bag sitting next to the bed, turned to JD and smiled.

"What do you want for dinner?"

———————

When I think about the people I know who have really loved me in my life, Mikey is one of them. When I said I wanted to travel to Peru to hike Machu Picchu, Mikey was the person who went out and bought the maps—actual physical, paper maps—so that he could research and study and plan our route. He planned training hikes for us in the Columbia River Gorge, and when my flight arrived in Lima later than his did, he went to the hotel to get our room, and then came back to the airport, so I wouldn't have to ride in the cab alone.

Over the 15 years we'd known each other, we'd been on dozens of trips together—road trips, hiking trips, skiing trips, trips to Jones' Creek to jump off the bridge into the icy water below. Sometimes he would show up at my door on a random Tuesday night and tell me to grab my things, because we were going to miss the sunset. Armed with a backpack full of beer, he'd drag me up the closest hill so we could find a good place to watch the sky explode into a thousand colors.

Mikey and I were always and ever only friends. Of course, I had wondered if we would ever be a couple. In one or two seasons, I fantasized about how, one day, Mikey would admit to me how much he'd always loved me and wanted to be with me. Then, in other moments—like right after another friend of mine committed suicide, and Mikey came over to lift me off of my floor and onto the couch—I would think about how I had never known a love like this. It was better not to spoil it.

This was why, when the argument erupted with JD about Mikey, I felt stuck.

It started when I asked JD if we could get together with Mikey for breakfast one Saturday morning. This was a tradition Mikey and I had—riding bikes to one of Portland's dozens of good brunch spots on a weekend morning and sitting for hours, talking and drinking coffee.

Mikey and I had talked about how things would change if one or the other of us met a significant other. We knew it wouldn't be like this forever. But if I was being honest with myself, I couldn't imagine life without Mikey. When I first met JD, I had a vision of him meeting Mikey for the first time, shaking his hand and saying, "Thanks for taking such good care of her."

But JD wasn't the slightest bit interested in getting breakfast with Mikey. In fact, he didn't really want me communicating with Mikey at all. It wasn't appropriate, he told me, for a pastor's wife—or anyone's wife, for that matter—to be spending so much time with a man who wasn't her husband. It was time to move on.

"Let's put the past behind us," he said.

I tried to explain to him why this was hard for me, how much Mikey meant to me, and how I wasn't suggesting things stay exactly the same. I only wanted JD to meet Mikey. Somehow in my stumbling, however, I mentioned that no one had ever really loved me like Mikey loved me, and before the words were even out of my mouth, I realized how they might sound to JD.

JD told me that if I wanted to marry Mikey, I should go right ahead and marry Mikey. But that if I wanted to marry *him*—meaning JD—Mikey wasn't coming to the wedding.

"Did Mikey buy you a ring?" JD asked, grabbing my left hand and lifting it up, so I could see.

"No." Mikey had not bought me a ring. I dropped my head into my hands.

Maybe JD was right. Maybe I'd gotten this whole thing wrong. Was I being unreasonable? Had I been confused about love this whole time?

This seems like a good place to pause for a minute and talk about love, since this is a book about love, and what it means to stay *in* love. One fear I've had in telling you this story is that you might think, when I say love, I'm talking about romantic love. Especially since so many of the stories I'll share here are about that kind of love, or include that kind of love. But if we get through this whole book, or get through our whole lives, and all we've done is figured out how to make a romantic relationship work, we will have missed it. The whole point. Our whole lives.

The thing with romantic love is it is such a good place to start, an incredible opportunity to talk about the larger function of love in the world. It's like a hand-hold, a way to talk about why love is so hard and so beautiful, and why we can't get enough it. If we can't figure out a way to love the people who are closest to us, if we can't figure out how to forgive those who have injured us most personally, how can we find a way to love or forgive anyone?

So as you read about JD and Mikey and all the other stories I'm about to tell you—as you make comparisons to your own relationships—I'd like to make one request. When I say "love," I'd like for you to imagine that what I'm talking about is a force in the world that is so supportive, so nurturing, so fierce, so committed to your purpose and full presence in the world that it will keep pressing until you wake up. Love is happening. You only job is to get out of the way and let it flow.

I didn't know any of this back then. I know it now.

After hours around the Mikey block with JD, I felt there was no way we were ever going to come to any kind of agreement. So I did something people do when they think they have to make love happen. I called Mikey. I told him we wouldn't be going to brunch, and that he wouldn't be invited to our wedding. In fact, I told him, this was the last time he would talk to me.

I felt JD's eyes on me.

"This doesn't sound like you," Mikey kept saying. I could hear the near panic in his voice on the other end of the line. I told Mikey this was a decision I was making, for my happiness, and that I was confident he would understand. He didn't understand. Of course he didn't. Not even I understood—and I was the one doing it.

When there was nothing left that either of us could say, we said goodbye.

When I hung up the phone, JD put his hand on my leg again.

"You did the right thing," he said.

I stood up and walked away. Even then, I knew I hadn't.

---

A few weeks later, the wedding day came and the music played and I stood there, staring down the glowing aisle, looking up at the face of my dad who was holding my arm, and down the way to the face of the man who was about to become my husband. A thought flashed through my head when I saw JD's face waiting there for me that I didn't have words for at the time, but if I had to give it words today, it would be this: *I don't even know you.*

Still, I smiled—because that's what you do on your wedding day. And I cried—because I felt sad and terrified and unsure.

"You ready?" my dad asked tenderly.

I smiled—and off we went.

We said our vows and danced and ate tacos and drank beer and left that night under a tunnel of sparklers on a pedicab. Strangers on the side of the street cheered at us as we rode down the streets of Portland on New Year's Eve. This whole thing should have been perfect. A *dream.*

But I was all twisted into knots.

# CHAPTER 2
# KEEP BREATHING

*"You were so afraid of my voice I decided to be afraid of it too."*
— **Rupi Kaur**

Sarah says the most important thing when it comes to yoga is your breathing. She says you can do yoga without breathing, but if you do, it's not really yoga—it's just sort of flinging yourself into headstands and handstands and whatnot. It can look good for Instagram, but what's the point?

Part of me wonders if this is a metaphor for life—how you can do all these really lovely, beautiful, impressive things, but if you're not breathing, not staying with yourself, not being honest about what's really going on inside of your heart, it's more like a frantic flinging than it is yoga. It looks good on Instagram. But think about how good a life can look on Instagram and how terrible it can feel to be the one living it.

I've been thinking a lot about this lately—about how for so many years I've been trying to do the "right" things, and about how all along

I haven't even been breathing. I haven't been honest with myself. Slowly but surely, I am learning.

―――――――

It was late November, just one week before Thanksgiving and only about six weeks before our fourth wedding anniversary. Hours before *episode three*.

We lived in Nashville, Tennessee, in a brand new house. I was working on a book about love and marriage. It was supposed to be about *our* marriage, actually—the challenges and the rewards. How relationships are what heal and change us. It was supposed to be a redemption story. Our redemption story.

I'll spare you all the details about how we got to Nashville, since you don't need them. But for the sake of understanding, it might be helpful for you to know that we had made three major cross-country moves since the first one from Portland, Oregon to South Florida. After a year at the church, we packed our things and moved to North Carolina. Then to Minneapolis, Minnesota. Then to Nashville.

So as I sat at my kitchen table, working toward my next writing deadline, there were a couple of reasons my hands were hovering over the keys but I couldn't move them. In addition to all the usual insecurities a writer faces, I was having a hard time figuring out how to tell the truth and also to say what I was trying to say. About love.

Something seemed *off*. Every time I went to write the words on the page, I couldn't do it.

Something I've learned, by the way, in the midst of this dismantling of my life, is that writing is diagnostic. Like yoga. It's impossible to be stuck in your writing and not also stuck in your life. Impossible to be stuck in your life and not also stuck in your writing. This is one of writing's many gifts. It shows us where love isn't flowing.

JD kept telling me he was *sure* I could do this, how this book was going to be my "breakout" book, the book that changed everything for us. But every time I would sit down to the computer to touch those keys, I would lock up. I was on the verge of giving up.

This, by the way, this "verge of giving up" thing, was a pattern for me. This up and down, passionate and devastating, emotional roller-coaster sort of a thing. This constant questioning and surges of inspiration would send me back to the page, convinced I had something I needed to say again.

A burst of laughter came from upstairs, where JD was on a conference call. Our Goldendoodle, Cooper, lifted his head where it was resting on my foot beneath the counter. I reached down to pet him gently.

JD and I had been working closely together since we met. Right away, he took on the role of my literary agent and manager, and was handling all of my website development and platform growth. He was good at it, always thinking of the next strategic thing he could do to grow my audience or make more money or sell more books.

Before JD, I was struggling to make ends meet, writing draft after draft of things and throwing them in the garbage. Now that JD was here, I was finally getting paid for my work.

JD was always saying I had the talent to really "make it" as an author. If only I could stop being so stubborn and dramatic.

I gripped my right shoulder, which was in constant pain by now. It had started four years ago, right after our wedding. At first, it was a small discomfort. Nothing more than a little kink in my neck. Over time it had grown to the point where, every time I sat down at the computer, I would get waves of pain down my arm, into my pinky finger—at times leaving half of my right hand completely numb.

I wiggled my fingers and reached for a bottle of Advil.

I turned my head from side to side, wincing at the feeling that shot through my body. I placed my fingers back on the keyboard. That's when it caught my attention, out of nowhere—his iPad, sitting there next to me on the counter.

---

Since we're telling the truth, I had searched through his messages a few times in our marriage. Secretly. One time, I found a short exchange between him and a mutual friend on Facebook, talking about a headache she had. He recommended she lay down for awhile—which sounded like him.

Then, later, he checked in to see if she was feeling any better, and it was the second part that struck me as odd. It wasn't awful. It just wasn't really *like* him. For all his strong suits, checking in to see how someone was feeling wasn't one of them.

This, by the way, was before I knew what I know now about how powerful our intuitions can be, how our bodies hold onto truths our minds can't yet understand, and before I ever trusted myself enough to stand my ground about something like this. So when I brought it up to JD, we talked about it for an hour—about why the messages bothered me so much, about feeling insecure, about how he was completely committed to me and to our relationship.

By the end of all of it, I felt like a real jerk, certain I'd overreacted about the whole thing. I apologized to him.

Then, on Halloween, MJ called in a panic.

MJ is my friend Mary, who I call MJ for Mary Joy, because along with Sarah, she is one of the happiest people I know. MJ is also my most composed friend—the one you call when *you* are falling apart—so when I heard the sound of her voice shaking on the other end of the line, I knew I needed to go to her house. I grabbed a sweater, said goodbye to JD, and climbed into my old Honda.

When I arrived, I found MJ in the kitchen with her sister and her sister's husband Ryan. MJ was flushed. I could tell she had been crying. Ryan was making chili.

I helped MJ and her sister set up lawn chairs outside, where the rain had broken for a bit. We grabbed giant bowls of candy, smaller bowls of chili topped with cheese and sour cream, zipped our coats, and carried little tables outside for our cocktails. Once we were all settled, I turned to MJ.

"What's going on?"

Between kids in cat costumes coming up to grab Snickers bars, MJ whispered to me the whole story. She'd been having an affair. It had been going on for awhile, but she had finally admitted it to her husband, Jeff. I shook my head.

"What's going to happen next?" I asked, breathlessly.

"I'm not sure…"

"Where is Jeff?"

"Out of town," MJ told me. They were both thinking about what they wanted to do and would reconnect in a couple of days. I told her I was sorry. So very sorry. And I sat there in the drizzling rain, eating chili and a tiny Snickers bar, thinking about JD.

When I got home that night, it was late. I walked in the door, and JD was on his computer. I asked him if we could talk for a minute. He said yes and looked up from what he was doing.

I sat next to him and told him I knew he was hiding something from me. I felt so calm as I spoke. I just knew he was hiding something, and I wasn't sure what it was, but that whatever it was, I could handle it. *We* could handle it. I could forgive him. I told him that, whatever "it" was, we could make it ok—as long as he was honest. This was the first time in *years* I felt peaceful as I spoke to him. The first moment I felt grounded, like I was standing on something solid.

For the first few minutes, he said nothing. He let me talk, and when I finished, he let a long silence linger between us.

Then he looked at me and said, "Look, I know you've been hurt in your life—but please don't take it out on me, ok?"

I nodded my head, stood up from our bed, and walked away.

It's interesting, because in light of everything I know now—everything I'm about to tell you in these pages here—remembering that comment should really make me angry. And for awhile, it did. But now I get it. Now I know there is only one thing that makes us lie and hide and run away. We are terrified of losing love. If only we knew there was no way to lose what has been ours all along.

––––––––

One morning, days before my wedding, I stood in the bathroom at my parents' house as the shower ran and the room filled with steam. Naked, I stared down at the ring on my finger and the most terrible feeling came over me, out of nowhere. I couldn't believe it. It was so horrible and so unexpected, and I did not want to be the kind of person who felt feelings like this. The feeling went like this: *I don't want to do this.*

I hated myself. Oh dear God, I hated myself. The invites were out. The plans were made. The tickets were booked. And he was such a good man. The best man I had ever known. The fog settled in around me. I tried to slide the ring off my finger so I could step into the shower, and for a minute it wouldn't budge. Frantic, I kept twisting and twisting and my breath became shorter and shorter and more panicked until finally my finger came free and I breathed a sigh of relief.

That's how I felt that day, looking at the iPad, right before *episode three* was about to happen. I could feel it. *Breathe*, I coached myself. *Just breathe.* But the thing about breathing and staying with yourself is that if you do it—if you really do it—eventually the truth will come out.

# CHAPTER 3
# WHAT TO DO WITH A BROKEN HEART

*"The truth will set you free... but not until it's done with you"*
**—David Foster Wallace**

'm sure you're curious what I found that day when I searched through JD's text messages. I could tell you all about it. All of the details. In fact, for a long time, I thought I would. Nothing was going to stop me from *finally* telling the truth. Especially after lying for so long. But the more I've thought about it, the more I have realized how easy it is to tell the truth about someone else and how impossible it feels to tell the truth about yourself.

Let's just say, for the sake of putting your mind at ease, that whatever you're imagining, it's worse. By that, I mean more heartbreaking. Whatever you think it is, multiply that times two, and you might be getting close.

But here's the real danger, I think, with spending too much time talking about this or thinking about it. You might get caught up thinking this story is about JD, when really it has only and ever been about me. The longer I work at this, the more I realize how often this happens. We get stuck thinking our stories are about someone else. We get lost in what's going on "out there" and miss what actually helps us to change, which is what's happening *right here*, inside of our hearts.

It's medicine—that's what Sarah calls it—all the pain and fear and horror that moves around inside of you when you let yourself really go there, when you finally stop focusing on everyone else and finally start seeing yourself. It screams at you. It is not so polite. But thank God it keeps screaming until you finally get it.

If I'm going to tell you the truth about *me* that day, I have to say how scared I was when I found what I found. More than angry. More than sad. I was scared. Scared of being alone. Scared of telling the truth. Scared of the fact that I had known the truth all along and had kept my mouth shut. Terrified of what this all meant for me: that I was finally going to have to start trusting myself.

It all shook around me and surged through me, and when I put my hand on my heart and my belly this time, it felt like something terrible and amazing might be happening. I wasn't sure what to do with it. Not yet.

*Medicine.* That's what I reminded myself. *It's all medicine.*

———————————

When I found what I found on JD's iPad, the first thing I did was leave. I ran. I grabbed a couple of things in flurry—a toothbrush and a change of clothes and my phone—and threw them into my purse. I put a leash on Cooper. On the way out the door, I stopped for a few seconds at the small hook inside the front door where our keys were hanging.

I didn't stand there long. I didn't rationally consider that, of our two cars, the Mercedes was the much nicer one, or that both cars happened to be registered in my name, or make a conscious choice to drive away in the Mercedes. I just did the only thing I knew to do in the moment. For just a minute, I trusted myself.

I grabbed the keys to JD's Mercedes, and stepped out the door with Cooper and with no idea where I was going. Twenty minutes later, I found myself at Don and Betsy's.

Don and Betsy were some of our first friends in Nashville. Aside from that, Betsy is the kind of friend you want around in a crisis: calm and measured and loyal, with the kindest heart. Not to mention, Betsy was one of only two people who knew about *episode two,* which I'll get to in just a little bit. I figured if I was going to tell anyone the truth, I wanted it to be her.

Betsy answered the door. She looked at my face, and then down at Cooper, who was standing with me on the porch.

"What going on?" she asked.

It didn't occur to me until I was standing there, looking at her confused expression, that I didn't have the slightest idea how I was going to say what I needed to say to her. No one had warned me how, when you spend so much time *not* telling the truth, the truth actually begins to sound quite unreasonable. You almost aren't even sure you're telling it. So I opened my mouth and said the only thing that would come out.

"Can I come in for a little bit…?"

Betsy was already ushering me inside.

———————

She put on a pot for tea, and I sat in one of the chevron chairs at the kitchen island, trying to decide where to start.

"Do you remember that time I went to Onsite?" I asked.

Onsite is a therapeutic retreat center about 40 minutes outside of Nashville. I'd gone for a week, several months earlier, right before *episode one,* back when I was convinced I was the main reason our marriage was not going the way I wanted it to go. I thought that maybe if I could work through my problems and issues and shortcomings, if I could get better at loving him, then maybe we'd be able to save this thing.

"We did this thing with horses..." I told Betsy, trying to find my words. "Equine therapy?"

"Yes, equine therapy. That's right. So the trainer who helped us with the equine therapy—her name was Jennifer. She was blonde and petite but also a total powerhouse, you know? Like, you could tell she knew how to put these horses in their place, despite the fact that they were ten times her size."

Betsy nodded.

"Jennifer introduced us to the horses and explained the whole thing to us; how we would pick the horse we wanted, and then spend some time trying to work with the horse in the pen."

I knew Betsy was familiar with this, so I didn't need to explain to her how horses tend to sense people's energy, and dealing with them acts like a mirror—a chance for you to really see yourself.

"There were two horses we could choose from that day. One was Hank, the other was Lightning."

"Ok," Betsy said, tracking with the story.

"I'm sure you can take a guess by the names which was the stronger-willed, more challenging horse."

Betsy laughed.

"Anyway, I watched as each member of my group went in with one or the other horse. First, it was Bo. He went in with Hank, the sweeter, softer horse. We all watched as Bo tried to move toward the horse, and the horse would back away. The harder Bo tried to get close, the harder Hank would try to get away.

"Crazy," Betsy said.

"I know. The trainer kept saying to Bo, 'you have to earn the horse's trust Bo... let *him* come to *you*.' Next was Leena. Leena chose to go into the pen with Lightning, since she had come to work on a relationship with her strong-willed fiancé. And I'm not kidding, within two minutes of Leena being in the pen, Lightening was bucking and rearing his head and just going completely crazy."

"You're kidding!"

"No, and it was the weirdest thing because when that happened, I was terrified. I kept thinking that horse is crazy and unpredictable. You never know what's going to happen next."

"So what *did* happen?"

"Jennifer asked if there was anyone else who wanted to go in the pen with Lightning, since he was already in there."

Betsy handed me a cup of tea.

"And, Betsy, it was like I was having an out of body experience. I heard myself volunteering to do it, even though I don't really want to. And part of me was like, *What the hell are you doing?* And the other part of me was like, *don't be such a wimp—he's just a horse.*"

"So what did you do?"

"I volunteered to go next. I walked up to Jennifer and told her I was ready. She told me I didn't *look* like I was ready, but I promised her I was. And then she said, 'You know, I think it is really brave of you to go in the pen, even though I can tell you are afraid. But I need you to know one thing before I let you go in there.'"

I looked at Betsy and paused, for dramatic effect. Or because I was stalling. Who knows.

"What was the one thing?"

"She said, 'if there is ever a time when you don't want to be in that pen anymore—if you feel like it's not safe for you to stay—you need to know you can leave. You leave anytime you want to. You hear me?'"

"So what did you do?" Betsy asked.

"I went in. I just acted like I wasn't scared and like everything was ok…," my voice trailed off.

"Is everything ok, Ally?"

"Betsy, I can't go back there…"

"To Onsite?"

"To my house."

---

"You seem so fine. How are you so fine?"

That was my friend Emily on the phone. I was driving again now, since this is what you do when all that energy gets stirred up in your heart—you fidget. You have a hard time sitting in one place for longer than a few minutes. You figure if you can just keep moving, you won't actually have to feel it.

I had just explained to Emily what I had explained to Betsy—*episode three*. What I'd found on the iPad.

"How do you seem so fine?" Emily asked again.

"I think I just took a wrong turn," I said, pulling a u-turn to get back on track. "Sorry, what did you ask?"

"I asked you how you seem so *fine*."

It's funny. I did not feel fine. I felt the opposite of fine. JD had called, wanting the Mercedes back. I felt like maybe I might be having an out of body experience. A heart attack? Everything was moving so slowly, and also so fast. I could hardly feel my face.

I thought about it for a minute. The only other time I could remember feeling like this was several years earlier when I'd been on a hike with Mikey through the Columbia River Gorge. We'd gotten stuck in the snow.

We were up just above Multnomah Falls, doing a 14-mile loop—over the summit and then back down the other side of the mountain. We'd parked our car in the lot at the base of the falls and knew we'd have to walk another mile on the road to get back to the car when we got out. So that would put us at 15 miles.

This was a training hike, since we were only a few months away from going to Peru to hike Machu Picchu. I'd done quite a bit of hiking, but Mikey had warned me I'd have to get used to hiking with forty pounds of equipment on my back.

"How does that feel?" Mikey asked me as he dropped the second of two big heavy rocks into my backpack and tightened the top.

"Feels like I'm carrying two big heavy rocks," I laughed.

It was raining when we started out—typical for the Northwest—so we were prepared for that. Plenty of layers and rain jackets. I left my cell phone in the car. Mikey brought his in a ziplock bag. Everything was going according to plan. That is, until the temperature dropped.

It's funny how things happen slowly, but also fast. When it started snowing, it was exciting at first. Not scary at all. Then, as it started to accumulate on the ground, I could tell Mikey was getting a little worried. I was cold, but ok.

"How are you doing?" Mikey kept asking every few minutes.

I kept nodding.

At one point, when we were up to our knees in snow, Mikey stopped us to get out the map. He wanted to try and calculate how much further until we reached the summit, so we'd know when our altitude was going to drop and the snow would turn to rain again. By this point, my fingers were going numb and I was starting to feel colder than I could remember feeling.

"Can we keep moving?" I asked.

We kept walking. According to the map, we would be at the summit in just a few minutes, which meant in half an hour, we'd be out of the snow for good. As soon as we started dropping down the other side of the mountain, though, the snow was not letting up and now we were up to our nearly our hips in it. Not only that, but it was impossible to see the trail, so Mikey was following the tree marks.

"Maybe we should turn back." Mikey said.

"Really? We're already more than halfway…" I was secretly lamenting the fact that this would make the hike longer than fourteen miles, which was already a stretch for me.

Mikey thought about it for a moment.

"Ok, you wait here. I'm going to go ahead and find where the snow tapers off. I'll call to you when I find it."

Mikey raced ahead to find the path, and I stood there waiting, listening to the silence of the snow falling around me, thinking about how strange it is that things can be so peaceful and also ominous at the same time. In a minute, I heard Mikey call to me, and I followed the sound of his voice. I had to barrel my way through waist-deep snow to get to him, but by the time I made it, he was on dry ground. Never have I ever been so grateful to set my feet on solid ground.

We kept hiking and talking and laughing the whole way at how much worse that could have been, and how cold we both were. It was raining and I was getting even colder now, but I kept telling myself we were almost done, almost there. At the end, we were meeting my parents for pizza and all would be well.

But as we rounded the corner to the last mile of the hike, Mikey stopped dead in his tracks. I came up behind him and when I saw what he saw, my jaw dropped.

It's a slow realization, you know? About how bad something has really become. It takes a minute for it all to sink in. What I saw was the river in front of me—raging wildly from all the snow runoff. So wildly, in fact, that the bridge we were supposed to cross to the trail on the other side had been washed out.

Mikey turned toward me. "We're trading coats. Mine is heavier than yours," he said.

I didn't argue. But when I reached my hands up to undo the zipper on my jacket, I realized I couldn't put my thumb and pointer finger together anymore. Mikey saw what was happening and reached to unzip my jacket. We quickly made the trade. Then, he turned me around and started taking everything from my backpack to put it into his. Except the two giant rocks, which we left in the woods.

He got out the map and unfolded it.

"What are you looking for?" I asked.

"Another way out of the woods."

A few very *long* minutes later, Mikey folded the map and turned to me, looking serious.

"We have three choices," he said. "We can go back the way we came. We can shimmy across this log and scale that rock wall on the other side of the river," he pointed to a huge log that had fallen all the way across the river to the other side, "or we can wrap ourselves in our emergency blankets and hope someone comes to rescue us."

I looked at him. This, for me, was when it really sunk in.

"Actually," he went on, "I take that back. Option number one is not an option. We can't go back the way we came. We'll never make it."

Never make it? Never *make it?* I told Mikey there was no way I was waiting in the woods to be rescued. We had little to no food, and I was already so cold I couldn't feel my hands or my feet. So it was settled. Mikey coached me on how to shimmy across that log. He went first and kept looking back.

"Take it slow," he said, over and over again.

Once we made it to the other side, we looked up at the rock wall we were going to have to climb to get back to the trail. It was probably 750 feet up.

"Good thing we spent all that time at the climbing gym," Mikey said, smiling, his sense of humor coming back.

"Good thing *you* spent all that time at the climbing gym," I laughed.

I had spent more time pretending to climb at the climbing gym than I had actually climbing. Lots of time standing back and "analyzing" other climber's strategies. Not to mention, my hands were so cold they couldn't even grip a zipper, let alone pull me up 750 feet.

"You'll be surprised what you can do when you don't have a choice," Mikey said, already pointing his eyes up to where we were going. I looked at Mikey. We started climbing.

Slowly and carefully, I put one foot in front of the other, looking for the smallest little handholds and footholds where I could make just an inch more progress.

"Great job. Keep going slow," Mikey said.

I reached for a handhold just above me and my foot slipped. I grabbed the first thing I could find to keep me from falling, which was a root sticking out from the rocks above. It was holding me, but I could tell it wasn't going to last long. I let out a loud yelp. Below me was a too-far drop back to the river we'd just shimmied across. I just sort of hung there, whimpering.

Meanwhile, Mikey leapt to secure himself on a rock above me. From there, he reached down, grabbed that backpack, and pulled me up to the ledge where he was.

I can't remember who started laughing first, but it was one of us, and then the other one started laughing because laughter is contagious, and it was like this uncontrollable, ridiculous thing because this whole situation was so horrible, and yet it was happening and here we were in the middle of the woods with no other choice but to keep going.

When we finally made it to the highway that night, it was dark outside and we were both smeared with mud and soaking wet and limping, and we still had that mile to walk back to our car. Mikey put his arm around my shoulder.

"I didn't think I was going to make it," I said.

Mikey smiled. "I mean, can you imagine how awkward that would have been for me at dinner with your parents?"

Suddenly I heard Emily's voice again on the other end of the line, which snapped me back into the present.

"Are you still there?" she asked.

"Yes, I'm here," I told her. I still hadn't answered her question—about why I seemed so fine.

"We fought about life insurance, Em."

"Life insurance?"

"Yes, life insurance," I told her. "A month ago we were in bed, and I turned over and asked him if we had a life insurance policy, in case something happened to him. I don't know where that came from, but all of a sudden I was curious, and I was thinking how weird it was that if we had a life insurance policy, I didn't even know."

"What did he say?"

"He said we didn't need a life insurance policy. He told me I'd be fine if something happened to him, and that I'd figure out a way to make it work."

I thought about Mikey reaching over and unzipping my jacket.

"What did you say?"

"I argued with him for a little bit, but then I dropped it. I knew it was never going to work to argue with him. He wasn't going to change his mind. So I just rolled over and went to bed."

There was a long pause on the line where Emily didn't say anything. "Emily, I should have known. That's the worst part of all of this. I should have known…" my voice trailed off.

"Actually, Ally—it sounds like you did."

---

When I stepped into the yoga studio that night, Sarah was standing behind the desk checking people in. I felt myself, again, wanting to tell her everything. Just everything. I knew she would understand. Instead, I signed my name on the sheet and without looking up, asked a question.

"Sarah, how am I supposed to do yoga with a broken heart?"

I wasn't just asking about yoga. I was asking about everything. How was I supposed to do *anything* with a broken heart? How was I supposed to keep breathing when it felt like the world was falling apart?

Sarah tipped her head to the side and looked at me with the softest eyes, so that my whole body felt like it might melt. Then she walked out from behind the desk and put one hand on each of my shoulders, looking me directly in my eyes.

"The better question is," she shook her head, "how are you supposed to do yoga without one?"

# CHAPTER 4

# WAKE UP, YOU'RE FREE

---

*"If I were going to begin practicing the presence of God for the first time today, it would help to begin by admitting the three most terrible truths of our existence: that we are so ruined, and so loved, and in charge of so little*

—Anne Lamott

P eople say that to get anywhere, you have to start where you are, but in order to do that you have to admit where you are, and I've always had a hard time doing that.

In a yoga class, for example, if you get too tired and out of breath, the thing you're supposed to do is to get close to the ground—back to child's pose. The idea is a nice one, if you ask me, that anytime you get overwhelmed, you just go back to the ground—to the beginning. You can start over. You can be a kid again. Think about how much time you spent as a kid laying on the ground, making snow angels or watching ceiling fans.

But if yoga practice is life practice, I have to wonder: Do we really get to take a break anytime we need one? Can any of us ever be kids again?

I tried it a few times—taking a break in the middle of a practice— but every time I did I would get this sinking feeling like I was failing terribly, just laying there on the ground while everyone else went on without a glitch. Instead of putting my head on the mat, like they tell you to, I would stare ahead, at the tall mirrors standing in front of you, wondering why no one else in the room needed to rest like I did. Why was I the only one who was losing my breath?

———

The first time I remember losing my breath in my marriage was the second night of my honeymoon. We were staying on the Oregon Coast, in a tiny little town called Manzanita. Some friends had offered to let us use their cottage, right on the coastline, which is wrapped up in the most beautiful fog that time of year. It's eerie and etherial and feels like you're in a dream.

We let ourselves in through the garden courtyard out front, and then through the front door, carrying luggage and groceries and movies and everything we needed for a long, slow, peaceful week. On the kitchen counter, we found several gift cards to restaurants and local shops, as well as a note from our friends that read *Happy Honeymooning.*

*Happy honeymooning.* It should have been obvious.

The next night we decided to go for a drive and use our gift cards. At our first stop, I found a pair of earrings I loved and used one of the cards to buy them. JD hung back by the door while I browsed, since the shop was full of mostly jewelry and handmade cards and, you know, refrigerator magnets. I really didn't think he'd want anything.

I could tell he was waiting for me though, so I hurried. And when I met him at the front door, he seemed upset. We left the gift shop and walked quickly back to the car.

When we made it to the car, I asked him if everything was ok, and at first he said yes. But then it became clear that, no, he was not ok and suddenly we were in an argument. Slowly at first, and then faster and faster, we fought until my heart was beating out of my chest. I kept trying to figure out what was happening and why exactly he was upset and what I could do to fix it, but nothing I tried was working. The harder I tried, the more frustrated he became, and the more frustrated he became, the more upset I felt.

I reached for my phone. That's when I remembered I didn't have it. We'd turned off both of our phones and left them at the cottage. I pictured a dinner with no texting and no Instagram and no emails, just the two of us. But suddenly, I realized that being here without my phone and in the tiny space of this car made me feel like I couldn't breathe. Oh my god, I *couldn't breathe*.

This was the first time post-wedding I realized I was drowning. Whatever reservations or fears I'd had before I married him were now multiplied, times ten. Like someone turned up the volume. Why did I assume all of this would dissipate after the wedding? What had I been thinking?

Here it was. The same feeling I had standing at the top of the aisle on my wedding day. Except now there was no way out. No turning back. What had I done?

Without thinking, without even *thinking* about it, the car slowed to a stop, and I unbuckled my seatbelt and got out. Got right out. I dropped my knees to the sidewalk, right there next to a stop sign, and put my right hand to my chest, just to try to get a full breath in. Tears were streaming down my face, and I was feeling like this was the most terrible thing that could be happening. This was the most awful thing

I could possibly do, getting out of the car, but I could not stop myself from doing it.

I tried to catch my breath. But by now, it was gone. Just way too far gone.

JD put the car in park and turned on his flashers. He waved to the drivers behind us, half as an apology, half as an instruction to tell them to go around us. Then, he came over to my side of the car and put his hand on my back. He held it there for a minute before saying anything. Finally, when he spoke, it was soft and gentle. Even apologetic.

"Don't do this, ok? Get back in the car with me."

The kindness in his voice infuriated me, since I wondered where on earth it had been a few minutes ago, when I was crying in the car. I feared his kindness was much more about avoiding the embarrassment of a wife on the sidewalk than it was about ending our argument. And I knew what would happen if I got back in the car. We would pick up just exactly where we had left off.

And still, I felt awful. The feeling was the same one I get in the yoga studio when I look in the mirrors and realize I'm the only one sitting on the ground, the only one in child's pose, the only one who has lost her breath. I felt like the biggest joke. Why couldn't I be stronger? Why didn't I know the right thing to do next?

I knelt there on the pavement for what seemed like a lifetime before I picked up my head to look at JD.

"Come on, get in the car," he repeated.

So I did.

What other choice did I have?

———————

You know, come to think of it, my honeymoon was not the first time I lost my breath with him. The first time was months earlier, just before we were engaged. I was in North Carolina meeting his family for the first time, and we had been talking about the fact that we would probably be married, although neither of us were exactly sure of the timeline.

"I have to be honest. I'm not moving across the country without a ring on my finger," I told him one day, knowing about his job at the church in Florida and thinking about the handful of friends I had known who had made major moves for significant others just before everything fell apart. What I meant to say was that I thought we should probably date for awhile before we made any big decisions.

"So what's your ring size?" he said, smiling.

I met his mom first. She came to the door, wrapped me in the warmest hug, and led me up to the bedroom that would be mine for the next few days. Next to my bed was a vase of flowers. I smiled when I picked up the card. *Welcome to our home,* it read.

"My dad wanted to make sure you got those," JD said, coming in behind me.

I came to the doorway where he was standing and wrapped my arms around him, thinking about how kind that was and about how kind his mom had been, and about how peaceful this house felt, how lovely and warm.

"I want your family to like me," I whispered.

"They're going to love you."

That night, a few hours after I finally dozed off in that bed that was not mine, I was shaken awake. It took me a good few minutes to figure out what was going on, but I sat up in the bed, in a panic. I looked at the clock—2:30 a.m. I could barely see JD's shadow in the dark, and my eyes were still blurry from sleep, but he was sitting next to me in the bed.

"Hey, I have a question for you," he said.

"What's going on? Is everything ok?"

"How did you get your guitar back from Ben?"

Immediately, I felt my stomach drop. I knew what he was asking.

Ben and I met at a summer camp when I was 18. That summer was such a beautiful summer, a blissfully happy last-summer-being-a-kid kind of summer. But summers come to an end, of course, and I was off to college that year, and Ben was off to his first real post-college job. I kissed him only once, standing by his Jeep, before waving goodbye. Then, nearly eight years later, we caught eyes across a coffee shop.

That connection between Ben and I was powerful. Visceral. The "love at first sight" kind of feeling you hear people talk about. I remember holding his hand for the first time and not wanting to let it go. *Was this it?* I wondered to myself. *Was this love?*

But of course, a few months into our relationship, I got the phone call. That horrible, awful phone call. I was in New York City at the time, doing research for a book, meant to be home in three months. But three months was too much time he said. He'd met someone. I tried everything to stop the unraveling on the phone that day, but it was too late. If what we had was love, it didn't matter. It was gone.

I had never known you could feel a heartbreak in your *body* like that. I laid on the floor for hours at a time that week, the week Ben called to tell me it was over. In an apartment that wasn't mine. It was a cold, hard, glossy wood floor, and all I wanted to do was stay close to the ground. Like a little kid.

After that, Ben and I saw each other only a few other times. Each were brief, since honestly, it was hard for me to be in the same room with him. The final time we saw each other was just a few weeks earlier.

I tried to make out JD's shadow in the dark of the night.

I had let Ben borrow a guitar of mine while we were dating. It was stupid. I don't even play the guitar, but he did, and I had this guitar my dad had given me as a gift, back when I was trying to learn. It had been in the trunk of his Jeep at one point, and I never asked for it back. It was elementary and immature and also human—this thing I had done. My way of holding onto something that was already gone.

One day, shortly after I met JD, I told him about the guitar and how it was time to ask for it back. This of course meant I would see Ben, which launched us into a bigger discussion about our relationship and my feelings for him. I tried to stay with myself, to stay with my breath. I really did. I tried to tell him everything—trusting he wanted to understand.

But the longer we talked, the more ridiculous I felt, about making a big deal out of any of it. JD suggested I have Ben drop the guitar on my doorstep. I didn't want to do that. But I wasn't quite sure why, so I didn't say anything. I couldn't explain. I felt pathetic about the whole thing. All the tears I had cried. All that laying on the ground I had done.

"So it's settled," I heard JD say the day we talked about it. "You'll call Ben and ask him to come leave the guitar on your doorstep."

"It's settled," I heard myself say.

Sitting there together, in the pitch dark of that room that was not my room, that bed that was not my bed, that home that was not my home, I felt myself barely taking in sips of air and barely letting them out. I was remembering what I had done. What I had told JD I had done, and what I had actually done—which was email Ben and ask him to meet me at a coffee shop.

We met at a coffee shop. He brought the guitar. We talked for 15 minutes. I asked if he was happy, and he said he was. He asked if I was happy, and I told him I was. I lost my breath. For just a minute. The truth was I was confused and conflicted and unsettled still, but I didn't want to be the kind of girl who was unsettled. I didn't want to be the girl on the curb, kneeling on the sidewalk. I wanted to to be the kind of woman who got back in the car.

After 15 minutes with Ben at the coffee shop, he left, and I knew this was goodbye for good. I was going to marry JD. I deleted Ben's number from my phone, but I didn't delete the emails where he and I had coordinated our coffee meeting. It didn't even occur to me.

I held my hand to my chest as we sat there, trying to steady my breathing, seeing a little more clearly now, seeing how JD was waiting for an explanation.

"Did you go through my email?" I asked.

"Why are you more concerned with how I know than you are with the fact you lied to me?"

That's what JD wanted to know. But I could hardly breathe. This was so terrible. I was so terrible. Why had I done this? JD kept pressing and pressing, and I just kept taking in tiny sips of air and trying to think of an explanation.

"Do you still love him?" JD demanded.

I wanted to tell the truth. I really did. But the truth was I didn't really know. What did that even mean? I didn't feel with JD the way I had felt when I was with Ben. Safe. Soft. Like *me*. Did this mean I loved Ben?

I supposed the answer was, *yes. Yes,* I still loved him. Do you ever really stop loving someone once you have started? But I could not bring myself to say the words because I knew what would happen if I did. Our whole relationship—this whole thing—would fall apart. I would never be able to make love work.

So instead, I lied. I swore to him that I did not still love Ben, that I just needed to get my guitar back, that the coffee meeting was short, uneventful and totally meaningless. Then I said one true thing, hoping this would satisfy JD.

"I needed closure," I said. "I needed to see him one last time."

JD couldn't understand.

For the rest of the night—until the sun came up—we sat there talking and trying to unwind the whole thing and I cried and shook and tried to breathe and tried to fix it. JD told me he might never be able to trust me again.

At one point, as the sun came up, JD said, "you know, part of me wants to put you on a plane and send you home."

I cried and I shook and prayed and prayed and prayed, *please, please, please don't let him do that.*

It's funny, looking back. I wonder why I was so afraid of that—of him putting me on a plane and sending me home. Why are so many of us working so hard to hold onto things we don't even want?

———————

"You have such an honest face," Sarah would say to me a long time later, after so much more had happened. We were in the yoga studio, laying on our backs, as close as we could get to the ground.

"What do you mean?" I asked.

"I mean you look so happy and free like this, without any make-up on. Your hair all wild and curly."

I had just come back from the beach, so I was wind-soaked and salt-stained. I felt like a mess. But at the same time, I felt like myself for the first time in a long time.

"It's the quality water," Sarah said. "Do you know what I mean? Like, when someone is so true, you can see right through them."

I nodded my head. I was getting better at deciphering Sarah's metaphors these days. There really *was* something about water. I flashed back to where I had been the past several days, sitting next to the ocean, listening to the waves. Soft, but also strong. One of the most powerful and, also, most gentle forces in the world.

"You know what you looked like when I first met you?" Sarah asked, turning to me.

"What?"

"A Christmas ornament."

"A Christmas ornament?"

"Yes," Sarah laughed. "Perfectly trimmed and manicured. Like I could hang you on a tree or something."

Now I laughed, too. I had spent hours staring at myself in the mirror in those days, picking and pinching and worrying about how I looked and what I was wearing and feeling so terribly flawed. All of that energy and attention to get something I didn't even want. Something that didn't even really exist.

"You know how I felt back then, Sarah?"

"How?"

"Trapped. All caged up. Like I was in prison."

Sarah nodded. "And now?"

I looked at her. Then back at myself in the mirror. And when I saw my reflection and my wild curls, I started shaking my head around until my hair was flying all over. Sarah followed suit. We both laughed and shook our heads until our crazy, messy hair was like confetti in the air. Like glitter.

It was beautiful.

---

The day JD proposed, we drove to the Oregon Coast and walked along the water, and I thought about how amazing the ocean was, how miraculous. In and out, in and out, over and over and over again. I was pretty sure I knew what was about to happen, since I had mentioned at one point that I wanted to get engaged by the ocean. But I pretended I didn't know because, somehow in my mind, this made the whole thing more romantic.

At one point he turned to me, and I knew this was the time. It was happening.

I took a deep breath and braced myself for what I expected to feel—that surge of love, that feeling of safety and surrender. But the surge never came. He got down on one knee and said the things you want a person to say, and the whole thing should have been perfect. Completely perfect.

But I felt nothing. I was all still and frozen and totally manicured and looking perfect. A woman in a cage. A prison.

# CHAPTER 5
# THE "RIGHT" THING TO DO

*"One day you finally knew what you had to do, and began, though the voices around you kept shouting their bad advice..."*
**—Mary Oliver**

I met a women several years ago who went to jail for murdering her boyfriend. I was volunteering for an organization at the time, working with women who had come out of addiction and prostitution. We had a task we were doing together, so our hands were busy. We both looked down as she told me what had happened.

She told me how, night after night, he had handcuffed her to the bed, beating her with one of those fire pokers. "What were they called?" she asked. Neither of us could remember the name. One night he held a gun to her head, and another night he broke a beer bottle and shoved the broken end into her wrist. She showed me the scars.

Then she told me, one time, he'd left the gun within arm's reach and she was high and tired of being his punching bag, so she just reached for that gun and pulled the trigger. I looked up from what we were doing and looked at her.

"You think I'm a terrible person, don't you?" she asked.

"I don't," I said.

I actually found her quite remarkable. In fact, I thought I probably would have done the same thing under the same circumstances. I surprised myself a little with that thought, but it was true. Because you can cage a woman for awhile. Her body at least. But there is only so long her soul will let her stay there. Alcohol helps. Drugs help. Any kind of numbing helps. But eventually the soul comes rising up like a fury, like a flood, and no matter what the circumstances are trying to stop her, her soul does not care. Souls are like that. Their *job* is to save us. They are unstoppable. Indestructible. Like fire.

---

It was December now and starting to get bitterly cold in Nashville. I sat in the waiting room of my therapist's office, wrapped in my warmest coat and tap tap tapping my foot to the beat of the elevator music. The colder it got, the worse my shoulder and right arm throbbed. It's amazing how much time I spent ignoring this pain, how much time we spend ignoring pain because we aren't sure what to do about it. I took my left hand and gripped tightly around my shoulder, to see if I could get the aching to subside for just a minute.

At one point, JD reached over and put his hand on my leg, his way of asking me to stop tapping my foot.

It had been a few weeks since *episode three*, and we weren't living in the same house anymore.

The first thing I did when he left was strip both beds in our house of all the bedding. I did it in a fury. Faster and more passionately than I had done anything in our entire marriage. I ripped the sheets and blankets and pillows and mattress pads from the beds—everything short of the mattresses themselves—and the only reason I didn't take those was I figured they were too heavy for me to carry. Then I grabbed all of it in three armloads and lugged it down to the dumpster in the back alley by our house.

With a stoic resolve, I drove to the closest West Elm and picked out brand new sheets. I picked the ones with the highest thread count I could find, found the softest blankets they had in stock, and chose colorful pillows to match the exact comforter I wanted, which was also the most expensive. I took all of those beautiful, soft, sturdy things to the cash register and set them down on the counter.

Without hesitation, I handed the woman my credit card.

The second thing I did was spend an afternoon canceling our fourth anniversary plans, which included first-class tickets to Cancun, Mexico. I canceled the appointment at the fertility clinic in Nashville, which I had booked months earlier. It was a giant unwinding, an unraveling— an undoing of everything.

I went to Thanksgiving at my friends' Katie and Tim's house. Katie's parents were there and a few other friends. Nobody asked about JD, either because Katie had prepped them, or because the look on my face said enough. They knew everything they needed to know.

It felt like I was dreaming, like my life was happening on a movie screen, and I was watching it happen to someone else. Not to myself.

I baked banana bread to bring to the Thanksgiving meal and made a sweet potato hash from scratch. That's what I *would* have done if JD had been with me. So I went through the motions. Then I sat at the table feeling as if someone had scooped me out.

I put my hands on my body the way Sarah coached us to do. I felt relieved and sad. Peaceful and furious. Resolved and undecided. Nobody ever told me you could feel two opposite things at the same time like that.

Every night I would lay awake in my bed—by myself, alone with my thoughts—only to realize the terrible way I felt about myself when I was with JD didn't leave the house with him. In fact, the most hurtful things he had said to me while we were together weren't half as bad as the hurtful things I was saying to myself as I lie there, alone.

*How could anyone ever love you?*

*You are such a joke.*

*You are nothing without him.*

In those dark, echoey, middle-of-the-night hours, I would lay there in my new beautiful sheets and think about how hard I had tried to do this right and how I had still messed it up. How was it possible for someone to try so hard and to get it so wrong?

I would cry with no tears those days. My body would go through the motions, my chest doing the heaving thing—up and down, up and down—but no tears would come. It was almost like I'd forgotten how to cry along the way. There was something surging under the surface, but I didn't know how to get to it.

When I sent an email to our therapist asking if she could meet with us, I was as vague as possible. I still wasn't sure what I wanted to do, I told her, but needed help deciding.

*I still didn't know what I wanted to do?*

That's how I wrote it at the time. It's crazy to look back and think about how much time I spent pretending I didn't know what to do, when the truth was I just wasn't sure I had the strength to do it.

Back in the waiting room, I was not tapping my foot anymore and my shoulder was still throbbing and there was the sound of a doorknob turning. Angela appeared.

"You two ready?"

We did not answer, but we both got up from our seats and followed her in.

We'd been seeing Angela off and on for several months now. Ever since *episode two,* which I'll explain in a minute. In order to understand *episode two,* first I have to tell you about *episode one.*

It was a Friday morning when JD called. He had been at a conference in San Antonio, and I had just come home from Onsite and my experience with Jennifer and the horses—the story I told Betsy that day in her kitchen. You give up your phone for the week at Onsite, so I hadn't spoken to JD in days. I arrived back home to find a vase of flowers on the counter and a note from JD telling me how much he had missed me while I was gone. Tears came to my eyes as I held up the note. Things were going to be different now. I was sure of it.

My certainty didn't last long.

The second I heard his voice on the other end of the line that Friday morning, I knew something was wrong.

"What happened?" I asked.

He told me the story, or as much of it as he could remember, which wasn't much. Still, it was enough. I tried to stay calm on the phone. I told him we would figure this out, that everything was going to be ok. I think I was saying it for myself more than I was saying it for him.

He did seem genuinely upset. In fact, it occurred to me I hadn't heard him like that before. I stayed with him on the phone for a bit. I asked him if he could come home early.

"I changed my flight," he said. "I'm coming home tonight. Can you pick me up at the airport at 8 o'clock?"

I agreed. But when I hung up the phone, I felt that same familiar, sinking feeling—like I couldn't possibly get close enough to the floor. I slid slowly down from the couch and all the way onto the hardwood, and laid there staring up at the ceiling, wondering how much pain one person should be expected to endure before it would all come to an end.

How was this possible? Why now? What was this all for? After everything I had just learned at Onsite—all the work I had done—it didn't make any sense. Things were supposed to get *better*, not worse.

I had no idea we were just getting started.

———————

"Who wants to start?" Angela said, snapping me back to the present moment.

Here we were, on this familiar couch, except everything felt different. Everything was the same and everything had changed. All at once. Angela looked to me.

"Since you sent the email, Ally, why don't you go first?"

Start. Ok, yes, I should start. I wanted to start. The problem was I wasn't sure *where*. Where had all of this started? How were you supposed to unravel something when you didn't know where it all started? How could you make progress without going all the way back to the beginning, to the ground, to child's pose?

My mind wandered back to that Friday night after episode one, after picking him up at the airport. We sat on our couch in our pajamas and went over details—the ones he could remember, which again, weren't much. I asked a thousand questions, and he did his best to answer them. He filled in some details from his co-worker, who apparently had a better memory of the evening than JD did.

It occurred to me as he was talking that he might not even be telling me any of this if it weren't for the fact that he'd been caught. And at the same time, I wondered if it mattered why any of us finally tell the truth, as long as we do it.

JD and I sat on opposite ends of the couch.

He seemed *innocent* sitting across the couch from me that night. Soft, actually. That was surprising to me. Because the truth he was telling me was terrible. It was quite awful, actually. Cutting. Disturbing in every way. But for the first time in all the time I had known him, I felt like I could see right through him.

He was clear, like water. Like Sarah says.

When we finished talking, I told him I needed him to sleep in the guest room for awhile, until we could figure out what to do next. I surprised myself with that request, since I hadn't had the courage to ask for anything like this in the past. I figured it was the strength I had gained during my week at Onsite, and also it was this softness about him. For just a minute, I felt like maybe I could trust myself.

JD complied.

Thriving off that momentum, I told him I was going to make an appointment with a therapist. I told him he didn't have to come, but that I was going to call and make an appointment regardless.

"I'm not asking your permission," I told him. "I'm letting you know this is happening."

I could hardly believe the words coming out of my mouth. But JD didn't move from his side of the couch. He didn't even flinch. He didn't get upset. He said he didn't like it, but that he would think about coming, and he wasn't going to stop me from making the call.

What came next was perhaps the most shocking thing of all. For the next six weeks, there was relative peace and happiness in our marriage. My therapist asked me once to recall a happy memory from my time with JD and to do it, I had to go here. Back to this six weeks. A blissful blip in our relationship. Lodged right between *episode one* and *episode two*.

One time during this blissful blip, he came into the kitchen while I was cooking dinner and put his hand on the small of my back. Another morning, I needed to run to the grocery store for tampons, and he offered to do it for me. Another time during this blissful blip, we sat on the couch making faces at each other, giggling. A few weeks into this time, I invited him back into our bed. We lay there on that first night, face-to-face, and I told him about a dream I'd had while I was at Onsite.

"I was stuck in the middle of the woods," I told him. "It was getting dark, and I was crying because I was freezing cold and I didn't know the way out…"

He listened to the whole thing, and then he reached toward me and tucked my hair behind my ear. "I would never leave you in the middle of the woods."

We had sex that night and didn't use a condom.

---

I've thought a lot about what to make of that night with JD, what to make of our blissful blip—especially with what came next. But the only thing I can think is that this was the real JD. This was the JD I wanted to marry. This was the JD I somehow always knew was in there. This won't make sense to you yet. Not until later, until you hear more of the story. But it makes sense to me now. In fact, it is the only way anything makes sense to me anymore.

This is what love does to us, I suppose. After all the suffering is over, it makes everything make sense.

Thank God.

What would we do without it?

---

"What would you like to do, Ally?"

Angela was asking. JD had been telling her all about what had happened, what I had found, and what had unfolded since. She'd asked JD what he wanted to do, and he said he wanted to fight for our marriage no matter what. He told Angela he was willing to do anything he needed to do to make it work. He had the most sincere look on his face as he said it.

But can I be really honest? I didn't believe him. Maybe he was telling the truth. But I didn't believe him. There was this terrible heat rising in my chest. I turned to JD.

"Do you remember the drive back from Atlanta?"

This wasn't like me, by the way, to bring something up like this to JD. *Episode two.* I knew he would know exactly what I was talking about.

It was six weeks after *episode one*, the still-fuzzy incident that had taken place at the conference in San Antonio. We took a trip to Atlanta for the weekend, for a friend's wedding. In fact, we decided to make a mini-vacation out of it. We rented a nice hotel room, and I packed lingerie and hid a pregnancy test in my purse because my period was now late and I was certain I was pregnant. As we drove, I smiled. I couldn't remember the last time I had been this happy.

The wedding was beautiful. It was fall in the south, and the weather was warm, and I danced with my shoes off. It was the smallest taste of freedom, the smallest taste of *me* that I had been missing for so long.

The next morning, I snuck into the bathroom and took the pregnancy test I'd brought. But when I heard the urine hit the water below, I looked down. The water was turning red.

My breath quickened. This couldn't be happening. I felt myself start to shake, slowly at first and then a little more, until I was crying—quietly so that I wouldn't wake JD. Shaking and crying in the bathroom by myself. Short of breath, I lowered myself to the floor and put my forehead against the cold tile. For twenty minutes I laid there, barely getting sips of air, trying to figure out what I should do next.

It wasn't the baby. Even then, in my grief, I knew it wasn't the baby. My house wasn't safe for a baby. My house wasn't even safe for *me*. And I think it was *that* realization that sent me to the bathroom floor that morning. The realization that no matter how hard I tried to muscle this dream into place, I wasn't going to be able to do it.

Maybe I would never be happy. Maybe I would never get what I wanted.

When I finally lifted myself to the shower, I turned the water extra hot. I let it run all over me. I let steam fill the whole bathroom.

We drove the first 30 minutes back to Nashville in silence. JD could tell something was wrong. But when he asked me about it, I told him I was fine. I kept staring out the window. I didn't want to tell him. I didn't think there was any possible way he could understand. I hardly understood myself.

Besides, I already knew what he was going to say. He would say that it was fine and I was blowing things out of proportion, as always, and that there was no reason for me to be upset.

But he pressed. He wanted to know. And the more he asked, the more I felt like maybe I should give him a chance. Maybe I was right that everything was different now. Maybe *episode one* had really changed him. Tentatively, tenderly, I told him about thinking there was a baby and taking the test and being sad and not knowing what to do with myself.

Sure enough, his response was what I expected. Now was not a good time for us to have a baby anyway, he assured me. We needed to plan for longer. We should probably go back to using protection.

I tried to hold it back. I really did. But there's only so long you can hold back a river of grief and pain and the lies that are holding things together. I could not control it any longer.

I started sobbing.

He reached his hand across the car, but the thought of him touching me then felt terrible. Perfectly awful. I could not let him. So I pulled away. This infuriated him, which made me cry even harder. Through the shaking and sobbing, I looked at him and said the thing they tell you is always the wrong thing to say in any relationship, unless of course you really mean it. I was so tired of hiding.

"I can't do this anymore, JD," I said. When I said it, I also slipped the wedding ring off of my finger and dropped it in the cupholder beside me. Clink.

That's when it happened—*episode two*.

He took the bottle of red Gatorade in his hand and, with one surprising motion, flung the contents in my direction. Gatorade went in my face and all over the window of the car, the seat, the center console, the dashboard, on my shirt, in my bra, on my jeans. In my hair. It even stained my underwear, which I would find, hours later, when I went to the bathroom. I dripped with gatorade and mascara and shook in the front seat of the car.

I wanted out. Out of the car. Out of this life. But how does someone get herself out of the life she has gotten herself into? How do you find your way out when you don't know how you even found your way in?

Angela cleared her throat again, bringing me back into the present moment.

"Ally, what would you like to do?"

I held my right hand to my stomach and my left hand to my heart. I wanted to answer. I did. But when Angela asked that question, one last memory played in my mind. One last time when I had lost my breath.

It was early December, a few weeks before our wedding. We were getting married on New Year's Eve and the plan was to get married at 8 p.m., celebrate until midnight, do the countdown with everyone, and then be off on our honeymoon.

One day in early December, JD pulled me aside. "Three hours is a long time for a reception. What if we leave at 11:00 p.m, and celebrate the new year on our own?" He gave me that look—the look a man gives his soon-to-be-wife about their wedding night.

So I agreed.

We announced the switch to my family, but they were confused. Hadn't I said I was excited about celebrating the new year with everyone?

Besides, the invites had already been sent out and people were expecting to stay until midnight. My sister wondered out loud what people would do if we ended the wedding at 11:00 p.m. on New Years Eve.

"The party can go on without us," JD told her.

"Have you ever known a wedding party go on without the bride and groom?"

That concern made sense to me, but the fact that I thought so frustrated JD, who insisted I told him I *wanted* to leave the reception at 11 p.m. Had I said that? I couldn't remember. When you get all wrapped up in trying to make everyone else happy, you forget what you did or didn't say. What *did* I want? And why was it everyone else seemed to know what I wanted when I didn't even know myself?

Then one day, weeks before the wedding, we were all in the living room. My family was in a semi-circle on one side of me. JD was on the other. Everybody was arguing—almost like I wasn't even there—about what we should do about the leaving time. I felt like I was in a fog, in a dream watching all of them. Listening to all of them.

All of a sudden, everyone stopped. All attention turned to me. The audience waited. The tension was thick, wrapped so tightly around me I could hardly breathe.

"What do you want to do, Ally?"

What did I want to do? What did I want to do? I didn't know. I felt empty, actually. Blank. Wide-eyed, I stood there. What did I want to do? What was the right thing to do? I couldn't decide. So JD put his foot down. Discussion over. We were leaving at 11 p.m.

The memory faded, and I felt JD's hand come across the couch and touch my leg.

"What do you want to do, Ally?"

I shook my head. I pushed JD's hand away. I felt like such a jerk for doing that, since he had that soft look on his face again. But for the first time in a long time, I didn't care. I looked at JD, and back at Angela. I was ready. It was time.

"I want a divorce." I said.

I wondered how long it had been since I'd heard myself tell the truth.

---

Angela tried to get us to keep talking that day, not to make any decisions too rashly. She reminded me there were options. There were other options besides jumping to divorce. But I wasn't listening.

I left Angela's office before the hour was even up. I drove straight to yoga at 6:30 p.m. I said hello to Sarah, and I set up my mat in the room, and I looked at myself in the mirror.

That night, I spent the entire class on the floor, tears streaming down my face. I didn't get up once. Didn't try for one single pose. I just laid on my back in that warm room and let the tears come. Finally. Here they were. My offering.

It was all I had. It was all it took.

Sarah came around about three quarters of the way through the hour and put her hands on my shoulders. When she did that, I opened my eyes and looked at her, upside down, since she was behind my head. She smiled this gigantic, soft, beautiful, electric smile. There was so much joy in her.

"I'm proud of you," she said.

I forced a smile through my tears. I wanted to believe her. But how could she possibly be proud of me? I was doing nothing, just laying here on the ground, melting. Not even the slightest bit of strength to get up.

# CHAPTER 6
# THE MYTH OF A GOOD WIFE

*"You do not have to be good.*
*You do not have to walk on your knees for a hundred miles*
*through the desert, repenting."*
**—Mary Oliver**

The funny thing about trying to be good is that the harder we try to be it, the less good we are. I'm convinced of this. The longer I watch this happen in the world, the more I realize that the people who are trying the hardest to be good have, for the most part, forgotten how good they already are.

Think about trees, who do not have to try hard to be what they already are. They just root themselves and ground themselves and shed their leaves and grow more beautiful with each passing year. Mountains do not wake up wondering how they can be the best kind of mountain in the world. They don't try to figure out a way to stand taller, or be deeper or wider or stronger.

They just stand there, shining.

Every morning they wake up and they do the same thing they did the day before. They do not compare this day to yesterday, do not compare themselves to oceans or to other mountains. They do not think about how they might be measuring up to all the other scenery around. They just are who they are. And think of how incredible, how remarkable, how totally magnificent they are, without even knowing.

All this fixing you've been doing of yourself, all this picking, what is it even for? What if it's all a big, beautiful, tragic distraction from how spectacular you've been all along?

———————

Someone told me somewhere along the way that, on average, a woman leaves an abusive relationship nine times before she leaves for good. That rings true to me, although part of me wonders if it might be even more times than that, given how many times she goes back in her mind. Back to the old way of doing things. Back to the old way of thinking about herself. That is the hardest part to untangle.

For weeks, after I made my declaration to Angela, I would lay awake in bed at night and think about all of the reasons why I couldn't do this. This was a terrible choice. The worst possible choice. A selfish choice. I could never make it work.

I would replay our first conversation with her—the very first day we sat on her couch. She asked me how I felt about divorce, and I told her I didn't believe in it.

"You don't believe it exists?" she asked, smiling.

"Of course I believe it exists," I said. "I just think people really have to fight to stay connected to each other, you know? I think love takes work."

Now here I was tonight, in bed, googling, "What are the divorce laws in Tennessee?" and "How do you find a good lawyer?"

One night, when it was too late to be on Facebook, I sat on my bed with my computer on my lap, looking for something to make me feel better about the decision I was about to make permanent. It's strange that I needed that, given that I had *so much* already. But when we look outside of ourselves for something or someone to validate our choices, nothing we find will ever be enough. Not even the most gargantuan validation will ever fill the well of self-doubt.

I searched through our bank accounts and through Facebook, clicking through pictures of women who were his friends. It wasn't long before I settled on a profile of a mutual friend—the one who'd had the headache, who had exchanged messages with JD earlier that year.

Feeling self-righteous and desperate, I typed a message to her. The general content of which was, "did you sleep with my husband?" Then, without stopping for a minute to even breathe, I hit send.

Almost immediately after I did it, I realized what I had done. I panicked, feeling around for a reset button or an unsend button or something to stop this flood of shame coming over me. But there was no way to undo what I had just done. Instead, I scrambled out of bed and threw on a sweatshirt and got in my car. On the way, I texted MJ. It was late January now, and she and Jeff were getting a divorce.

I texted her on the way. *OH MY GOD, I've done something terrible, I am coming over.*

When I got to MJ's house, she was up making flower arrangements for a baby shower she was hosting the next day. She met me at the door, and we walked into the kitchen. For the next two hours, I sat with her at the kitchen counter, sipping the cocktail she made me and cutting flower stems. I told her everything.

I clipped geraniums while I repeated the story—the story of sending the Facebook message, and everything that had led me there. My knees were drawn up to my chest on the stool, and I was talking a thousand miles per minute. At one point, when my cocktail was almost gone, I held one of the soft flowers in my hand. I looked down at the blossom.

"MJ, why did you do it—sleep with someone else?"

She took a deep breath, as if she had so many things to say but didn't know where to start. She tucked another flower into the arrangement she was working on and shifted everything around. Then she looked at me. She shook her head.

"This is not your fault, Ally."

I dropped my head into my hands. Until she said it, I hadn't realized I felt like that. I hadn't realized how much I felt like a fool. A failure. How could this *not* be my fault? How could I not make him love me? I had given him everything. What a terrible realization to realize that even *everything* you had to give was not enough.

"I feel like such a joke," I said.

"You're the opposite of a joke," MJ said. "You are a *force* to be reckoned with."

I shook my head. I wasn't sure how that could be true.

MJ and I talked for another 30 minutes or so, and I helped her with the rest of the arrangements. I thanked her for letting me come over and she walked me to the front door.

"No more late night Facebook messages, deal?"

"Deal."

But later that night, about an hour after I made the promise, I broke it. Except this time, I sent a message to Sarah. I wrote it all out. I told her that this was out of the blue and that I wasn't even sure why I was telling her all of this, but I told her everything that had happened. All of it. My whole heart.

At the end of the message, I said to Sarah, "I have this constant pain in my right side that won't go away. For some reason I thought you might be able to help."

Sarah and I met on a Tuesday. It was a rare snow day in Nashville, so I put on my warmest coat and boots and walked to her house, which I discovered was .2 miles away. We both walked together to a tiny little hole-in-the-wall taco spot in our neighborhood.

When we walked through the door of the restaurant, Sarah did this thing she does often, which is to throw her arms in the air and let out the loudest laugh. Everyone within a 10-foot radius turned to look at her. She didn't seem to notice.

"Whatever drugs you're on," I told her, "I need some."

We ordered at the counter and sat at a tiny table in the back of the room. A small neon sign hung right over her head, flickering a bit, and snow fell softly out the window.

"I read your story," Sarah said.

I nodded and took a sip of my horchata, feeling awkward now that I had unloaded this entire thing onto a stranger.

"Sorry to do that to you."

"Don't apologize. It's a beautiful story."

I looked up, and Sarah tilted her head. She did this often, with this look on her face like she was asking you a question you should know the answer to. She lifted her right hand and put it on her belly, and her left hand and put it on her chest, over her heart. I mirrored her.

"Do you think I'm pathetic?" I asked.

"To think that, I'd have to think I was pathetic."

*Tacos for Ally,* the loudspeaker boomed.

I slid out from the table to get our food. As I walked to the front of the restaurant, I felt the tiniest bit sad that I had said that thing about being pathetic, since I was seeing now how thinking I was pathetic wasn't any different than thinking she was pathetic. Now I got it. My story was Sarah's story. Not the exact details. But she understood.

I returned to the table and set our tacos down in front of us. A sweet potato taco and pork taco for me. Chicken tortilla soup and a sweet potato taco for Sarah.

"You're strong, you know that?" Sarah said before I could even sit down. "So strong."

"I tried, Sarah. I really did."

"Of course you did."

"I wanted to be a good wife."

"You were the *best* wife, bunny. You fought harder than most people would. You can be done proving yourself now, ok? You can let it go."

"Do you know what grace is?" she asked.

Part of me felt like it should be easy to answer that question, since I had grown up in church, where we talked about grace all the time. But now that I was sitting here staring down at my food and not feeling hungry at all, the only things that came to my mind as I thought about grace were images of letting JD come back home—and I knew I couldn't do that.

"I don't know anymore."

"Grace is really two things. The first is the ability to endure the unendurable. Congratulations. You've already done that."

I looked up from my food, intrigued.

"And the second?"

"The second is about making space to receive blessings. That's where you are right now. You're in a place where you are trying to make some really good, healthy, clean space for blessings. Letting go. You're doing good work, bunny."

I reached up to grab my shoulder, which was throbbing more than usual right now. Sarah took a minute and swallowed her bite.

"I can help," she said, nodding to my right side.

It's funny, since this was exactly what I was hoping for, exactly what I had come here wanting, and now that she was offering it, it felt hard to receive. I could feel myself resisting, worrying about what it would mean to say yes.

"Why, Sarah?" I asked.

"Why what?"

"Why would you help?"

"Oh, sister," she said, shaking her head, as if I should know. "Helping you is helping me."

That was what did it. What tipped me over the edge. As I looked at Sarah now, for the first time, I realized I saw myself. A mirror. All the joy in her eyes, that was my joy. All the pain in her eyes, it was my pain. All the truth and softness and fierceness and fire—it was all mine.

It was ours.

Sarah put her hands on her body again, and I followed suit, and that feeling that I was empty now dissipated. There was something to me. Some substance. I wasn't alone in this. I didn't have to do this by myself. And maybe—just maybe—like Sarah and Robi and MJ, I was a force to be reckoned with. Maybe, just maybe, this could be my way forward.

I hoped Sarah was right about all of it.

---

One thing I'm learning is that when you think you are at the end of yourself, you are quite often at the beginning. Rock bottom is a remarkably sturdy foundation from which you rebuild your life.

All winter in that yoga room, we did the most unthinkable things— laying on our backs, with our legs to the sky, straight up. Sarah would turn on the music really loud, and then we would begin criss-crossing them, from our thighs, over and over and over again, for three full minutes, faster and faster and faster. The room would fill with steam and the mirror would drip with sweat and until our entire bodies would shake like earthquakes, like volcanos about to erupt.

My face would turn bright red, and I would melt into my mat, and Sarah would remind us that if we wanted to get strong, this was how it happened. If we wanted to change, this was how change took place—all the heat and all the fire and all of the shaking. Bolts of lightning. That's what Sarah called us. *Bolts of lighting.*

I shook and melted and crumbled and fought and cried in that room all winter. I tried to let it all happen—me, getting strong. That was my mantra. *Strong, strong, strong.*

You do the best you can in a yoga practice. You give it all you have. You fight and hold postures even when your body shakes because you know shaking means you're growing. Then, when it's all over—when you've done all you can do—you lay on the ground and you let it all go. In yoga, they call this *savasana*. Total surrender.

––––––––

Sarah and I started meeting regularly at the studio, just the two of us. She would have me lay on my back or sit in child's pose and she would softly adjust my shoulder with only a few fingers, gently pressing into my shoulder and neck and back.

"How does that feel?" she would ask.

"It feels fine."

One day, after spending most of our hour on the floor, Sarah had me lay flat on my back and pull my right leg up to my chest. Then she had me lift my left leg, just a little, and bounce it in the air, moving my heel to each side of my mat.

"Ok, switch legs," she said.

I did the other leg. This was the only effort I had exerted in our entire lesson, the only time I'd done anything other than just lay there. So when she stood up and asked me if we could schedule another meeting, I was surprised.

"Is that it?" I asked.

Sarah smiled, as if she could read my mind. But instead of answering, she answered my question with another question.

"Do you know the only reason we do the strengthening we do in the bigger class?"

I thought about it for a minute.

"I guess I don't."

"It's so we have something sturdy to hold onto," Sarah put her hands on her body, the way she always did. "Something solid to stand on. When you have a strong core, then you can open your heart. Basically the only reason we get strong is so we can be soft."

Strong and soft. I nodded, slowly. We booked another time to meet, and I walked out the door.

―――――――――

I stopped working on the book. I realized I didn't want to do it anymore. I hadn't wanted to for a long time. I started sending emails and cancelling all of my speaking engagements. Any travel in January and February, I just decided I wasn't going to do it. I deleted almost everything from my calendar, making space.

I booked a ticket back to Portland so I could be with my family for Christmas. One night, I went out and bought a Christmas tree with lights and ornaments and set it up in my living room. The room was mostly empty now, but when I set up the tree with all of the lights, I stood back and thought about how it actually looked kind of warm and peaceful in there. I smiled. It wasn't much. But it was enough.

I was shocked, at first, by how gentle this all was. I would go to the hot yoga room, and we would still hold planks, or try to push ourselves up into handstands, or shake and tremble, or try. But I would meet with Sarah, and she would just barely touch the base of my neck. She would knead it gently, like dough, and I would feel something small happening. Something so beautiful and small with the most unexpected ripple effect.

There was only one thing on my calendar I didn't cancel. Something with JD in January. We were filming a video series. This had been on the calendar for months, and we'd already spent a good bit of money to get ready for it. Most of our revenue in the coming year was going to come from this one project. Most of *my* revenue, I corrected myself. It was taking some time to get used to saying that.

*I can do this*, I told myself. *Strong strong strong. I can pull myself together. I can make this happen.*

January came, and I drove to our office to meet JD and the team. I got in the elevator and let it lift me to the fourth floor. I stepped inside and felt that familiar feeling, like I was living in a dream. Like the world was moving around me, but I was not part of it. There was a flurry of motion waiting—cameras and people and hair and make-up. JD was standing there, at the elevator. This was the first time I had seen him since that day in Angela's office.

He smiled.

"Thanks for being here. It means a lot to me," JD said.

There was one part of me, if I'm being honest, that liked the feeling of being there. It felt familiar and good and normal. JD was happy. *I can do this*, I thought. *I can make this work. We don't have to let go of everything, just because we are getting a divorce.*

But another part of me watched as everyone moved through that room with purpose and intention, and I suddenly felt like maybe this was some kind of alternate reality. I turned to JD.

"What did you tell them?" I asked.

"What do you mean?"

"I mean what did you tell them about us?"

JD paused. I could tell my question caught him off guard. We'd worked with this crew before, and they were our friends. None of them were acting like anything was different.

I shoved my hands in my pockets.

"What would you like me to tell them?" JD asked.

I smiled and nodded. This was getting easier and easier.

"I have to go," I said, smiling.

"You have to go?"

"I have to go."

JD tried to talk me out of it. He seemed sincere that day—so genuinely sincere when he said he would do whatever I needed him to do. He would tell the crew whatever I needed them to know. But it was too late. I was already on my way out the door.

I rode the elevator down, laughing to myself and thinking about how gentle it could be. Grace. Making space.

---

A few weeks later, on a Wednesday, I filed for divorce. That day was just like any other day. I woke up and made a pot of coffee. I cut up an apple and spooned a bit of almond butter onto the plate next to it, coaching myself to eat something, even if it was something small. Around noon, I climbed into my car and drove downtown. I drove. I parked. I rode the elevator.

Just one step at a time. One thing at a time.

The divorce attorney shook my hand and introduced herself. She offered me coffee or water as we walked back to her office. We sat down at her desk—her on one side, me on the other.

"I'm here to file for divorce."

It was such a small thing, those five words. Just such a small, gentle thing, whispering the truth.

The whole meeting was surprisingly short. Maybe 15 minutes. Then, when it was all over, she handed me a packet and told me to be in touch if I thought of anything else. I felt so small as I walked out those big, giant, swinging doors. So incredibly small.

I rode the elevator down, down, down, walked down the hill to the library and back to my car. I waited to feel something. Something terrible, something different. But I felt nothing.

*Strong strong strong. A force to be reckoned with.*

A week later, when the discovery documents came, I scrolled through the questions they asked about our marriage. None of them phased me—had I had any extramarital affairs, did I have a problem with alcohol. Then, I got to a question about halfway through the list that just about stopped my heart. It said, simply: *Was she a good wife?*

I sat there for 30 minutes at least, wondering how he would answer that question.

I thought about that day on our honeymoon, when he had come over to my side of the car and gently coaxed me back in. I had done it, the thing a good wife does. I thought about *episode one* and how I had agreed to keep the whole thing between us. He was sorry enough as it was, and there was no point in making him feel more embarrassed.

I thought about calling Mikey and telling him he wouldn't be invited to our wedding. I thought about packing those three boxes with my things and leaving everything else behind. I thought about my wedding day, about pretending to be ready, even though I wasn't.

Suddenly I felt it start to boil up in me. Fury. So much anger. For the fact that I had worked so hard to be *good*, I'd forgotten to be my beautiful, remarkable, miraculous self.

Oh, what a good wife I had been.

I just didn't want to be one anymore.

# CHAPTER 7
# COMING UNDONE

---

*"Most things will be okay eventually, but not everything will be. Sometimes you'll put up a good fight and lose. Sometimes you'll hold on really hard and realize there is no choice but to let go. Acceptance is a small, quiet room."*

**—Cheryl Strayed**

I wish I could say that was it, that this was the turning point in my story, that everything steadily got better from there. I wish stories went like that. I wish healing worked like that. But, I'm learning, healing is slow. So painfully and excruciatingly slow. Sadly, we do not magically wake up one day to a changed life. We have to keep showing up to our pain, over and over again.

And just when you think you've let go of everything you could ever possibly be asked to lose, you find you still have your fingers wrapped tightly around those few tiny things you loved the most. Surrender does not always come quite so gently.

I know this now. I didn't know any of it back then.

———————

February came, and the temperature dropped into the 20s in Nashville, which felt unusually cruel. I pulled a hat over my ears and stepped out into the biting, unforgiving cold of the morning.

In my hand was the police report, as well as the card the officer had handed me the night before. Detective Hummel. *Hummel. Hummel.* I rolled that word around in my brain a few times and thought about what had happened in the past 24 hours.

I'd gotten an email from JD around 6:00 p.m. the night before, asking if he could come over. It was his turn to take Cooper, who we had been passing back and forth. My heart was pounding when I read the email. It was so familiar. I couldn't explain it. And still for some reason, I found myself typing, "Yes, I'll be here until 7:30 p.m. You can come get him any time."

I closed my eyes for a minute, thinking about it. About why I kept letting myself do that—saying things that were not true and doing things I did not want to do. I thought about how much room JD took up in this house, even though he didn't live here anymore. How much space he took up in my life, even though he wasn't in it.

When he arrived at the door, there was something about the look on his face and the way he was standing that made me double-take. I had seen this look before.

I took a few deep breaths. I was blowing things out of proportion. Surely I was making this up. And still, even as I told myself this, I found myself backing away slowly, as if my body was moving without my mind's permission. I had Cooper by the leash by the front door, along with the bag of all of his things, since I had planned to hand him over easily. But now we both backed slowly away from the door where JD stood. One step after the other.

"What the hell are you doing?" JD asked.

It wasn't until he spoke that I realized I had literally backed myself all the way into the living room, caddy corner from the front hallway. This was the furthest away from him I could possibly get—and it wasn't far enough. My heart was still racing.

He asked for Cooper, but I wouldn't hand him over. This didn't phase JD. In fact, now he was laughing, telling me that I could act like this for as long as I wanted to—but that he wasn't leaving the house, and I wasn't leaving the house until I gave him the dog.

At one point, he picked up his phone.

"She won't give me the dog. No, I'm standing right here at the house, and she won't give me the dog."

My phone wasn't close by. It was sitting there on the counter—in my line of sight, but too far to reach. I felt my heart rate rising as it became more and more clear how this was going to work. I played all the possible scenarios in mind, but knew if I didn't do something quickly, I was going to regret it.

I sat there on the couch with Cooper, his leash still on him, all of his things waiting in that bag by the door. I wrapped my arms all the way around his sweet body, knowing that if I let him go now, this would be the last time I would ever see him. And yet also strangely sensing this was the only option left.

I hugged Cooper for the last time, and I let him walk to JD.

———————————

Weeks earlier, JD had come over to get the rest of his things from our house. The whole thing was like a funeral procession—stuff laying all over the back deck, where our storage unit was, and all over the the floor, and all over the couch. We tried to decide together whose was whose, what was what. But how do you divide something that cannot be divided? How do you split something that cannot be split?

We unpacked and packed and moved in a sort of silent agreement of surrender. When we had finally made all of the decisions and loaded everything into his trunk, we stood at the front door saying goodbye. Not even touching.

"I want you to have it," he told me.

"Have what?"

He looked around, from the stoop of the house and waved his hand up in the air and all the way around.

"All of it. You deserve it."

When he said that, I softened. There was a small part of me that wanted to reach out and touch him. I wanted to ask him if there was a way to unwind all of this, to fix it, to undo the damage we had done. Instead, I fought back tears and looked around at all we had built and wondered why the thought of keeping it all didn't make me feel any better. What I wanted most had been gone for a long time.

A few days later, I called JD and told him I didn't think I could handle loosing Cooper. Actually, what I said was that I could handle losing JD or losing Cooper, but not both. Losing Cooper was the part that made all of this feel unbearable.

"Don't do that," JD said.

"Do what?"

"Pretend like you're sad about this," JD said. "You are the one who is making this decision."

I hung up the phone feeling like maybe JD was right about everything. Maybe this was all my fault. Maybe I deserved exactly what I was getting. I hated this. One day I would feel one thing, and the next day I would feel something different, and hated that I couldn't get my bearings on myself.

I would go to yoga and hold my shoulder, which sometimes felt like it was getting better, and sometimes felt like it had never been worse, and think to myself about what Sarah had said about grace and letting go. What if I let go of everything, and it didn't help? How much could one person be asked to lose?

Even if this was the only way to get out alive—the letting go—how was I supposed to survive it?

---

Something about it didn't feel right—showing up at this place in the Mercedes, his Mercedes. Or was it my Mercedes? It felt like a betrayal, if I'm being honest. It felt surreal, as if I was playing a character in a movie but not living my real life. Still, I thought about what my attorney had told me the night right after JD left with Cooper—to call the police—and about what the officer had recommended I do when he stood at the door, writing the report.

I got out of that car and walked silently inside.

The waiting room was about like you would expect the waiting room to be at the Domestic Violence Center of Tennessee, except that's a strange thing for me to say, since I had no idea what to expect the Domestic Violence Center of Tennessee would look like.

"Ma'am, may I help you?" The receptionist was looking at me through her plexiglass shield, from behind her desk that, if you ask me, was taller than it needed to be.

"Oh yes. I need to file a… uh…" I cleared my throat. "I think I need to file an order of protection?"

"Ok. Fill out this paperwork."

She handed me a clipboard, and I nodded, taking a seat in one of those way-too-stained-for-comfort hospital waiting room kind of chairs. I looked at the questions. Name. Social security number. Date of incident. Police report number. Officer's name. Complete description of the event. I held my left hand to heart, gripping the clipboard.

I filled out the top portion of the paperwork, copying the number from the police report the officer had handed me, and finally I did my best to tell the story from the night before, sticking to the facts as best as I could. The fluorescent lights flickered above, and I could feel myself getting a headache.

I stood up and handed the clipboard back to the receptionist. I smiled at her when I did that, and she smiled too. When I sat down, I looked to my right and saw a woman sitting there, holding an infant in her arms, wrapped warmly in a tiny blue blanket. I smiled at her, too, wondering if she noticed how dark my eyes looked. She smiled back.

I glanced up at the receptionist again.

Suddenly, out of nowhere, this felt like a terrible idea. I never should have come here.

My heart started to race as I thought of how I could get out of there. I could tell the receptionist I had changed my mind—I'd had a temporary blip in judgement, or that I was just waking up from some sort of sleep-walking-type episode. But just as I was playing out that alternative scene in my mind, I heard a voice from behind me.

"Ma'am?"

I looked up from where I was sitting. There, standing above me, was a man, nicely dressed—in a shirt and a tie—and darker skinned than me, with an accent.

"Let's step into my office," he said.

I followed him back to his office, which was really just a cubicle with a card table in it, covered in documents and files, and with two more chintzy chairs like the one I'd been sitting in out in the waiting room. The fluorescent lights still flickered, and I felt grateful I hadn't put any make-up on that morning. I rubbed my eyes.

"Can you tell me what happened last night?"

I considered reminding him that I had written it all down, and that he could just read what I had written, but since the paper where I had told my story was right in front of him, I assumed he knew that and for some strange reason he was still wanting me to tell the story again.

So I told him. I repeated all the events as slowly and carefully as I could, unemotionally. I told him about the emails JD and I had sent back and forth. I told him about JD coming over to my house, and about seeing that look in JD's eye—that familiar look—and about telling him I didn't want to give him Cooper.

I told him about backing away, and about how he stood in the doorway, arms crossed, saying, "I'm not leaving until you give me the dog."

I told him about calling my attorney, and following her instruction to call the police, and then about how Officer Jackson had filed a report and told me to come here.

When I said that, I flashed back to standing there at my front door, with Officer Jackson. He'd been so kind.

"Have you ever filed a police report before?" Officer Jackson asked, and I had shaken my head. No—this was the very first time I had ever called the police. The very first time I had ever filed a report. And the very first time it really hit me how many times I *should* have done something but never did. Why had I never done anything before?

"Ma'am, are you still married?"

That was Detective Hummel now. We were still sitting here at this tiny little card table.

"I've filed for divorce, but..." I paused. "Yes, technically we are still married."

"And is your husband's name still on the title for the house?"

I nodded.

He wrote himself a note.

"I need to ask you," Detective Hummel said. I could tell he was speaking carefully. "Were you afraid for your physical safety last night?" I stared at him—eyes wide, head shaking back and forth a little bit, heat pulsing through my entire body. I leaned forward in my chair, still wrapped in my down jacket, which made a swishing noise as I moved.

"You have to understand, detective," I started, "that in the past four years of my life, I've been so afraid for my safety so many times."

"I understand," Detective Hummel said. "But ma'am, I have to ask you again. Were you afraid for your physical safety last night?"

Silence hung heavy between the two of us. The only thing you could hear was the sound of the ticking clock, and the slow swishing of my coat as I took deep breaths in, and then out, and then in again. Tears burned at the back of my eyelids. I held back.

"Because, you see," he continued, "I'm concerned about what might happen if you try to file for an order of protection with the story exactly as you've written it. You're still married, and your husband still technically owns the house you're living in, and what you've written here doesn't make it clear that you were afraid for your physical safety. I can help you file for this restraining order, but I have to warn you the judge might not grant it."

"So what are you saying?"

"I'm asking you if you felt afraid for your physical safety last night."

There was so much I wanted to say. Instead, I pictured myself taking my arms and shoving every last thing off of his messy desk. All the stacks of paper—just flinging them across the room. That stupid photo of his wife and two sweet boys sitting on his desk... I pictured myself picking it up and throwing it against the wall into a million pieces. Screaming.

Did he need proof that I was a woman who had lived through hell? I would show him.

Instead, I just sat there, silent and resolute, as I had so many times in the past four years.

I couldn't look at him anymore. It might as well have been JD sitting across the table from me. All I could do was look at my feet. Look at my hands, which were shaking now, and white because of the cold. My breath was getting short, and my face was hot.

"This was a mistake," I said, shaking my head. "I never should have come here."

Detective Hummel shifted in his seat.

"I'm not saying you should leave. I'm just saying that if we do this, you're going to have to stand in front of the judge, and you're going to have to tell your side of the story—so will your husband—and the judge is going to want to know if you felt afraid for your physical safety."

I stared at him. I thought about standing there with JD again, his story against my story. I couldn't do it.

I stood to leave.

"If anything comes up, or if you have any problems at all, or if he comes back... call me. Or call the police. Anytime. Document everything, ok?"

He handed me his business card. I took it and held it in my hand. I got in that stupid black Mercedes, and I drove home.

---

I stopped on the way home at Home Depot and bought new locks for the house. When I got back in the car, I called my friend Melissa and asked if she and her husband Mike could come over and help me change them.

"We're on our way," she said.

Mike changed the locks on every door in the house, and I made tea and told both of them the whole story. They listened and said they'd go back with me if I needed them to, that they'd do anything they could to help.

"Honestly, I think I just need to let it go."

"Are you sure?" Melissa asked.

Strangely, I was.

In fact, as I thought about myself standing at the domestic violence center, and pictured what Detective Hummel told me I would have to do to get the permanent order of protection—stand in front of the judge with JD, telling my whole story—I realized the thing I needed more than anything else was to never have to do that again. To never have to fight with JD again.

Now that he had Cooper, there was nothing left for him to take from me.

I knew what this meant—this walking away, this letting go. It meant I would never see Cooper again. It meant I would never see or speak with JD again.

"I wish I would have done this sooner, Mel. I wish I would have woken up sooner."

"You're doing it now," Melissa said.

And suddenly, I realized why I *hadn't* done it sooner. Letting it all come undone. The reason I had fought for so long to hold this whole thing together wasn't for JD. It wasn't because I was such a great wife. It wasn't for our marriage. It was for me. It was so I didn't have to feel this feeling I felt right now. I wasn't sure I could do this.

After Mike and Melissa left, I laid on the floor for an hour. I heaved and sobbed and let sounds come out of me I didn't even recognize. I let it all come undone. I let everything crumble until I couldn't possibly have cried anymore tears, not even if I had wanted to.

And then I laid there, feeling weirdly peaceful for a second, because the strangest thing happens when everything falls apart. You finally don't have to hold it together anymore.

# CHAPTER 8
# MORE LOVE, LESS FEAR

---

*"When I run after what I think I want,*
*My days are a furnace of distress and anxiety;*
*If I sit in my own place of patience, What I need flows to me,*
*And without any pain.*

*From this I understand that*
*What I want also wants me,*
*Is looking for me…"*

**—Rumi**

One of the things I have loved about yoga is there is nowhere to hide. In life we hide behind all kinds of things—make-up or name brands or job titles or last names or relationship statuses. In yoga, in that hot room with all those sweaty not-so-covered-up bodies, there is nowhere to go except right there. In the truth. The fleshy, terrible, magical, beautiful truth of you.

February came and went, and I kept going to yoga and meeting with Sarah. Sometimes it felt like we would spend more time talking about love and broken hearts than we would spend actually doing yoga. When I told Sarah this, she looked at me.

"Bunny, what is yoga if it's not healing a broken heart?"

So I would sit there, in whatever pose Sarah instructed, and let her gently coax me deeper into the pose. Meanwhile, I would tell her the story of how one time, I'd accidentally left my computer bag at a Starbucks, and how angry JD had gotten about it and how I hadn't known what to do to calm him down.

I felt myself get really upset about the whole thing, just furious at him for making such a big deal out of something that did not seem like a big deal to me.

"I kept apologizing and apologizing, Sarah. But no matter what I said, he would not forgive me."

I let myself come totally undone about it there on the floor. Even before that memory was complete, I thought of something else.

"One time we were on a plane flying home from Oregon. My dad had just had open heart surgery, so JD and I flew home to be there. It was the first time I had seen my family in a long time, and JD was accommodating that week. He would drive to pick up food or sit next to my mom and sister and me, with his hand on my leg. He took care of everything."

"Then, on the flight home, we bumped into one of my dad's friends, with his wife, and the two of them asked how my dad was doing. Do you know what JD did in that moment?"

"What?"

"It was late—a red eye—and we had first class seats. JD got up from his seat and went to tell the gate agent that we wanted to give our seats to our friends, and that we would sit in coach."

Sarah looked at me, searching my expression.

"What am I supposed to do with that?" I asked, shaking my head.

It was so confusing. That was the hardest part about sorting through all of these memories—some of them were so confusing. I went on. The memories kept coming.

"I was at the grocery store the other day and I picked up this bag of grapes, Sarah, and it was the craziest thing. Suddenly, I was transported to another place. It was like someone kicked me in the back of my knees. I found myself on the ground, like an idiot in the middle of the grocery store, crying."

"What did the grapes remind you of?"

"One time when we were first married, I pulled a bag of grapes out of the refrigerator. We were getting ready to go and I wanted to take some with me. JD was upset I wasn't hurrying, so I started rushing around, just sort of flinging myself around without a plan, and I forgot the grapes were on the counter. Five minutes later, I still wasn't ready to leave, and when he called to me from the other room, I didn't answer him. That's when it happened."

"What happened?"

"He picked up the bag of grapes and he hurled them at the wall."

I felt my whole body respond when I said that.

"He was strong, Sarah—so strong that the grapes exploded everywhere. I remember staring at the wall, just amazed at how much of it was covered with grapes, my heart racing. There was grape juice and grape skin and grape flesh—the meat of the grape, you know—*everywhere*. It was like a grape massacre."

Sarah laughed.

"But I sat there on the ground of the grocery store for a good three minutes probably, barely breathing, before I could stand up. You know?"

"Oh, I know."

She asked me to turn on my back now, and she lifted my right arm above my head and she felt around for a minute before putting her thumb in my armpit, finding the exact spot where the tension was, and pushing just a little. It was just the tiniest bit of pressure but I gasped.

"Breathe," she told me.

I was shocked. I hadn't even known that was there—whatever it was. How had she found the exact right spot?

"We hold all of this stuff in our bodies, you know. All the fear. All the grief."

"That's crazy, Sarah."

I sighed a few times, and she coached me to keep breathing. Sensation shot through the entire right side of my body.

"We come to yoga for three reasons," Sarah said. "Do you know what they are?"

I shook my head.

She pressed her hand even more deeply into my armpit now, until the pressure and the sensation in my right side went from about a five on a scale from one to ten, to a seven. Sarah went on.

"First, more love. This practice teaches us how to be more love, to find more love, to have more love. Second, fear. Yoga helps us release our fears, face our fears, get over our fears. And third, more of what we want in our lives. Yoga gives us a greater capacity to manifest what we desire."

I nodded. More love, less fear, more of what we want in our lives. That sounded nice. I hoped she was right about that. All of it. I hoped it was possible. I hoped it wasn't too late.

"I've been teaching yoga for a long time now, and no matter who I meet—how old or how young or how disheveled or put-together, their story is always the same. It's always some version of this: I have loved, I have lost, and I am here to heal."

"Do you think everyone can heal?"

"Everyone who keeps showing up, heals, Ally. I've seen it a thousand times. But here's the thing. People stop showing up when they stop wanting to change."

That made sense to me. It wasn't easy, this constant process of showing up. Of admitting the truth about yourself. This experience of letting the heat and the pressure move through your body. I could see why people wouldn't want to do this, why I had waited so long to do it, and why it would be so easy to throw in the towel and give up.

When Sarah was done pressing her thumb into my armpit, she lowered my arm and that's when I felt it for the first time—the most incredible release. A beautiful relief. Like a melting of something solid. A softening. Sarah put her palms gently on my shoulders and coaxed them a little closer to the ground. Oh so gently, I felt it opening. My heart. My color bone. My chest.

What a sweet release. Like a wind tunnel, an echo chamber, suddenly I felt oxygen coming into places where it had not been for a long, long time.

––––––––––

The thing about space is that once you have it, you have to decide what to do with it. Most of us are terrified of this, I think. Marianne Williamson says that the spiritual life is not a life without drama, but it's a life without *cheap* drama. I think we're terrified of what a life without cheap drama would be. What would keep us occupied?

What might it be like to have openness in our lives? What would we do with the echoey emptiness? How would we find our purpose if we had nothing to prove? No one who needed saving? Then, we'd have to face ourselves.

By March, I would drive around town and see the smallest pink blossoms coming back to the trees. I thought about how incredible it was that the trees knew how to do this each winter—that they die and then come back to life. What an unbelievable feat they would undergo every single winter. A re-birth.

One Tuesday in early April, my friend Kate showed up at my door holding a cup of my favorite coffee and wearing her best purple power-suit. Today, my divorce would be final. She offered to drive me to the courthouse and to be moral support.

My friend Beth—in her four-inch black boots that went up past her knees—and Kate stood like oak trees next to me, strong and steady. They sat while I waited outside the courtroom, and while I sat inside, and while I answered each one of the judge's questions.

"Would you like your maiden name back?" the judge finally asked, his last question.

I said yes. And that was it.

"You should feel really good about this," my attorney told me as we walked out of the courtroom. "You got a great settlement. It's time to celebrate."

I knew she was right. Beth and Kate agreed. But as we walked out of the courthouse, I couldn't explain the feeling I had. Now I could go home and close the door on all of the drama, fear, and storminess of the past years of my life. No more moving. No more arguing. No more running from the house. The strangest sensation came over me. Now what would I do? Now what was left?

I drove home that day and sat in the silence of my house, all alone. I should have have let Kate and Beth stay with me for the day, since they both offered. Instead, I went into my house and locked the door and laid on the floor, staring at the ceiling. It was dark, and a little chilly, and quiet.

Since there was nothing else to do, I scrolled through Instagram. If I had known what I was going to see that day, I never would have done that. If someone had warned me, I would have done anything else. A book. A movie. Anything. Thank God I didn't know. If we knew absolutely everything that was going to happen before it happened, we wouldn't do any of it. Any of the totally amazing, totally stupid, totally miraculous things we do. And then—oh wow, how we would miss it. Everything we ever wanted. Thank goodness for all that we don't yet know.

There it was. Right on Instagram. JD with his new girlfriend, in the Bahamas. She was beautiful and in a swimsuit, and they were holding glasses of champagne and also each other, gushing about how this was real love. There it was, the life I had lived for so long, right in front of me. It was not even mine anymore if I had wanted it.

It was as if my phone leapt out of my hand.

Dropping it on the living room floor, I rushed out the front door. I held my hand to my heart, the way Sarah would have us do in yoga class, and felt it racing, beating so hard. The sound of waking up. The sound of saving your own life. How incredible is this? No matter how far we've wandered from ourselves, the most valuable thing we've ever owned has been with us all this time.

When the crying slowed, I picked myself up off of that front stoop and walked over to Sarah's. Sarah opened the door and welcomed me in. We sat on the couch, and she made tea and I told her what I had found. She listened to the whole thing.

"Do you sort of hate her?"

"Sarah, I *am* her. I am the girl in that picture. I can't hate her. I also can't be her anymore."

She nodded.

"I can't go home," I said, shaking my head. "I don't know what to do. Why now? It doesn't make any sense. I can't bring myself to go back into that house. It's a terrible place where all of those terrible things happened. I can't go backwards."

"So what are you going to do?"

"I don't know."

We both nodded. She said I could stay there for the night if I wanted, while I figured out what I was going to do next. I held that warm cup of tea in my hands, and suddenly, I felt something.

"Sarah, what if I am nothing without him? What if, when it's all said and done, I'm nobody? What if I'm nothing?"

"I guess there's only one way to find out."

―――――――――

There's this line in Moby Dick about getting to the ocean. He's talking about growing grim about the mouth, when it's a damp and drizzly November in his soul, and how when he feels that way, he finds it high time to get to the sea. As soon as possible.

That night, sleeping in Sarah's guest room, I could not overcome the urge that I had to get to the sea. As soon as possible. I needed to be close to the ocean. It didn't make any sense, but I was getting there now. I was starting to trust these little urges I would get. Thinking about my house and how much I did not want to go back there, I pulled out my computer and did it. I booked a one-way ticket to California.

# CHAPTER 9
# ALONE IN A GARDEN APARTMENT

---

*"Sometimes it takes darkness and the sweet confinement of your aloneness to learn anything or anyone that does not bring you alive is too small for you."*
**—David Whyte**

I arrived at LAX late at night and climbed in an Uber and watched the city pass by as I rode to my little garden apartment. I'd rented a little place on Airbnb, and I'd rented my own house out at home as well, to help me cover the cost of my trip. I had a little bit of work to do here and there, but I could spend time alone, read, write, drive to the beach, go to yoga. Whatever I wanted.

I re-read the instructions of the Airbnb as I rode in the Uber. *Green garage. Code to the lock. Key in the back closet. Black gate. Garden walkway.* The city flashed by in the window, and I tried to imagine what the next four weeks would look like.

We pulled up to a huge, green garage door, and my driver helped me get my suitcase from the back. Then, in an instant, he was gone, leaving me on the dark street. I stood there with all of my things, staring up at my little garden apartment. This was it.

*Here goes nothing*, I thought.

*Here comes everything*, I heard Sarah's voice say.

I found the key, made my way to the big iron gate and struggled to unlock it. I tried to hold the heavy gate open with my foot, while I wrestled a giant suitcase up the steep stairs. This was of course easier said than done. The gate crashed in on me several times before I was able to wiggle the suitcase through the small opening and up the stairs, one at a time. Halfway there, I stopped, out of breath, and looked around.

Two men walked by, laughing and talking loudly, coming from another apartment and pushing past me to the gate.

"Sure, I'd love a hand," I whispered to myself as soon as they were out of earshot.

Hot pink flowers cascaded down over the cement ledges above me, and crickets were loud, and the moon was bright—although not quite bright enough to illuminate the path through the garden. Sweating and struggling, I finally got my things up the stairs and made my way through to the front door. When I finally unlocked the dead bolt and fought my way inside, I collapsed on the couch. It was quiet. Very quiet.

I lay in bed alone that night, listening to the sound of crickets and people passing by outside. What was I doing here? I was alone, and everything was quiet, and I could hear the sound of my own thoughts, and this was just *terrible*. What had I been thinking, coming all this way? Oh my god, this was a colossal mistake.

These late at night hours are the worst for grief because your thoughts start to run away with you. You get on a particular thought about nothing really, except it won't let you go. It runs away with you, all the way down it's sinister dark path, until it drives you crazy. That's what was happening with this line of thinking.

*If I wanted to be alone*, I told myself, *I could have done that in Nashville. What was I thinking?*

*If I had wanted to drink coffee and sit around all day, I could have done that at home.*

I was getting quite stern with myself, giving myself the hardest time. I tried to focus on breathing—in and out, in and out—trying to get my heart rate to slow. And just when I felt like I might be getting close to falling asleep, I heard voices outside the window. At first, I thought I might be imagining things. But sure enough, they kept closer and closer until it almost sounded like they were inside.

I stayed perfectly still.

"You're impossible!" I heard the man say.

"Jason, I'm still not sure what exactly I did…"

"You're kidding me."

Wide-eyed, I sat up in bed and peered out the window. The streetlights illuminated the two of them. He towered over her, trying to get her to give him an explanation for whatever it was she had done. She sunk to the ground on her knees. Then she stayed there on the pavement, gently sobbing.

"Get a grip on yourself," the man said.

She tried to collect herself and he stood there watching her. Then he spoke again.

"You're a disaster. I'm going home."

Without any further explanation, he turned and left and she was just left there, sobbing on the sidewalk.

I scrambled to find a pair of flip flops in the mess of my suitcase and rushed to the front door of my little garden apartment. I don't know what I thought I was going to do. Fling open the door and rush to… what? To rescue her? By the time I made it to the front stoop, I didn't even have to decide. Because at that point, a memory came over me so powerfully I could not move.

It was a fight we'd had shorty after we were married. At the crescendo of the thing, when it had already gotten so ugly you couldn't imagine it getting much uglier, he said it.

"You were such a *mess* before I met you!"

I was frozen in space, as if this was happening all over, in real time. I sat myself down on the front stoop and closed my eyes. I felt it. *All* of it. The same kind of sensation I'd felt in the right side of my body when I laid with Sarah in the yoga studio and she pressed her thumb into my armpit. The heat, the burning, the shaking, the purging of something.

I sobbed with her—this girl I didn't even know. With only a garden between us. I cried, and I shook, and I cried some more, not because of what JD had said to me that day during our fight, but for the first time, I realized I had believed him.

What a terrible, beautiful, miraculous place for a person to be, alone in a garden apartment.

When the crying slowed, I picked my head up from my hands and looked around. I lifted myself from the stoop carefully, dusted off my backside, and more peacefully this time, went back to the bedroom. I peered out through the window to see if my crying friend was still there, but she was gone.

This time, I fell asleep easily.

------

On Tuesday night, I drove to my friend Noah's house to pick him up for dinner. He flung open the door, as tall and handsome as ever. It had been nearly five years since I had seen him, but his tight, dark curls were exactly the same as I had always remembered. Not to mention his bright smile. He scooped me up as soon as he saw me, lifting my feet off the ground.

"How have you been?" Noah asked. "I want to know everything."

Noah is the friend I worked with at the restaurant in the Pearl District, who wandered the streets with me, memorizing poetry. He was also one of the handful of friends JD asked me to stop talking to when we got married.

"It's not appropriate," JD had said.

"But JD, Noah is *gay*," I emphasized.

"It doesn't matter. Gay or straight, I don't want another man texting my wife heart emojis and telling her he loves her. It's not fair to me, and you know it."

Did I know it?

I peered over Noah's shoulder. From my place by the front door, I could see out the sliding glass doors onto the back deck, where the sun was about to set over an aerial view of LA.

"Oh my God, let me give you a tour!"

Noah grabbed me by the hand and walked me around the house, which was at the top of a hill in Echo Park. He walked me through the living room and the bedrooms, all of them wide and sprawling with the most beautiful wood floors. When we made it to the kitchen, he offered me a drink. He poured us each a glass of wine.

"Cheers," he said, lifting his glass to mine.

"To being friends again," I laughed.

"Yes ma'am, to being friends again."

Next we walked through the dining room and out those sliding glass doors onto the back deck, where he had set up a table to do his writing.

"Noah, this is incredible!" I said, throwing my arms into the air, breathing in the warmer temperatures.

We walked to the edge of the deck, and I took in the view.

"That's the observatory right there," Noah said, pointing toward the horizon. "If you get a chance while you're here, it would be great for you to hike there."

"Remember how much we used to love hiking in Portland? I miss that," I told Noah.

"Me too."

I held onto the railing. The last time Noah and I had talked had been two weeks before my wedding. I was sitting in the living room. JD was sitting next to me. He had coached me on what to say to Noah over the phone, and now he was sitting there, listening.

Noah took a deep breath, which brought me back to the present. He put his elbows on the railing and looked out over the edge. That's when he said it.

"What happened, Ally?"

I had thought about what I would say if was ever given this opportunity. The chance to apologize to Noah. There were so many things I wanted to say. But somehow, in that moment, my mind went blank.

"It wasn't my choice, Noah."

"No. No way. That's not fair. That's not *you*, Ally. I need a better explanation than that."

That response was so *him*, it weirdly felt like no time had passed since we'd last been together. I shook my head and smiled. After another few moments of my silence, Noah spoke again.

"Do you want to know what I think?"

"Of course."

"I think you wanted to be loved so badly, Ally. You did. You wanted to be loved *so* badly that you did whatever you had to do to get it."

I shook my head in disbelief. He was right, as much as it hurt to admit it. What a strange, terrible thing I had done—to trade all of these people who loved me for someone who wanted to be my husband.

Noah looked at me with his blazing eyes, so serious and gracious and mature. The light was painting the sky now, exploding into a million colors. Pink and blue and purple and magenta and orange.

I gripped that railing tightly and looked out over the edge, knowing if I turned toward him, I would lose composure.

"Have you talked to Mikey?" Noah asked.

"I tried. Days after JD moved out of the house, I emailed him. He was the first one. Then I tried to find him on Facebook. I don't think he's interested in talking to me."

Noah nodded. I held my hand to my chest, feeling the beating of my heart and wishing I could go back and do everything over again.

"I've lost my way, Noah."

"You're finding it."

"I am?" I asked.

He wrapped his arm around my shoulder, and I laid my head on his chest. The earth was about to swallow the sun whole now.

Noah turned to me, his face shining with the light of the sun.

"I'm proud of you for doing this month alone thing."

"It's terrible, Noah," I laughed. "I mean truly awful. It's been a day, and I'm already miserable."

"This is the way we find ourselves in grief, Ally. In the silence. When we get quiet and we sit still, and we learn how to be who we have always been."

I wanted to ask him what happens if we realize who we have always been was the problem in the first place, but I didn't. Because this moment was sweet, and I was thankful to be here with him, even if just for a second. I didn't want it to end.

Noah broke the silence, speaking in that reassuring tone of his.

"Hungry for tacos?"

"Oh Noah," I laughed. "It's like you've known me for ten years."

---

On Sunday, I woke up with a strange urge to go to church. This was out of character for me. I hadn't been to church in almost two years now. JD stopped going a short time after we arrived in Nashville, and I stopped going shortly after that—mostly on account of the fact that church was a terrible place to go all by yourself.

Still, that morning, for some unknown reason, I could not get this idea off my mind. So I peeled myself out of bed and got in the shower.

I showered and dressed and grabbed my things and left the apartment, locking the door behind me. I found a church on Google Maps and drove straight there. But when I parked my car, it was the strangest thing. I couldn't get out of it.

It was quiet in the car. Everything outside was muffled. Like watching a television show of a life that is not your own. Slow motion. Dulled and blurry and far-away sounding.

I sat there watching families and couples and people dressed beautifully, looking happy and purposed, walking toward the building. I kept wondering if they were really as happy as they let on, or if they were miserable, like I had been, and they were just smiling because that is what you do when you go to church.

I spent a good twenty minutes trying to talk myself into going inside, but realized eventually that no matter how long I sat there, I was not going to be able to do it. Instead, I put my car in reverse and pulled out of the parking lot.

---

I drove and I drove, not sure where I was going to go. I was feeling all frustrated now, and anxious, and stirred up—even a little pissed off. Maybe it was what Noah had said, or that feeling of sitting in the church parking lot and feeling like such an outsider.

I had gone to church my *entire* life. I had done all the things. Done my best. Married a pastor. Followed the formula. And none of it had given what it promised.

Ten minutes later, I pulled off to the side of the road into a place where it looked like people drank at eleven o'clock on a Sunday morning. *If you need me, you know where to find me,* I said to God bitterly on my way in. *Feel free to send an angel or something.*

I walked inside and sat at the counter and ordered a vodka with soda water and a lime. Suddenly I wished I had brought my bigger purse, which always has a book tucked inside of it. I needed something to do with my hands so I didn't have to just sit there, feeling like a loser. I stared at the TV mounted to the wall, pretending to care about whatever sporting event was happening.

On my right were two men—probably in their late forties—talking and drinking and laughing. To my left was a woman, about fifty, drinking a glass of Chardonnay.

"What's the score?" she asked.

"Huh?

"I'm Stacy," she said, smiling and reaching for my hand.

I felt a little disappointed, honestly, since I hadn't come in here looking to talk to anyone. But for just a minute, I laughed to myself considering Stacy might be the angel I'd told God to send if he wanted to find me.

She motioned to the bartender for another drink. I wondered if angels are allowed to have more than one glass of wine.

"What brings you here?" Stacy asked.

"You mean I don't look like the kind of person who spends her mornings in bars? I'm offended."

Stacy laughed.

"Well, I'm recently divorced," I said extra dramatically. "Visiting LA for awhile. I guess I needed to get out of town."

"Ah, yes. I'm divorced too," Stacy said.

"Really?"

"Yes. Twice."

I winced at the thought. I couldn't imagine being divorced more than once. The one time was enough for me.

"Where are you from?" Stacy asked.

"Nashville."

She nodded and we both looked back to the TV. I pretended again to watch what was happening.

"I used to go to church on Sunday mornings," I offered without looking away from the game. "My husband was a pastor."

"Really?"

"Yeah." I held up my empty glass to the bartender, indicating I needed another.

"And now?"

"Now I sit in bars talking with strangers on Sunday mornings, apparently. I don't know. I'm still trying to figure it out."

Stacy smiled. "Aren't we all."

"Hey, can I ask you a question?"

"Anything."

"Do you ever feel like it was all your fault? Like, you know it *wasn't* your fault, but then you get alone and you worry it *was* your fault and you think about how, if you were the problem from the beginning, then you might just be doomed to do this crazy-making thing all over again?"

Stacy looked at me.

"Dear, you're talking to a woman who has *done* the crazy-making thing all over again."

I nodded.

It was the strangest thing. For just a second, for just the slightest second as I sat there spinning the ice cubes around in my glass, I didn't feel as alone as I had a few moments earlier. It was amazing, really, this sensation that despite the fact that I was here in this strange place with this person who was nothing like me, she was everything like me.

"Ok, so another question for you," I laughed. "I might as well, while I'm at it."

"Shoot."

"Why does a woman marry a man she does not love?"

Stacy paused.

"A woman marries a man, my dear, who wants her about as much as she wants herself."

I kept drinking and drinking. Stacy paced herself. We talked about all kinds of things, most of which I don't remember. Then Stacy told me about her daughter, who was almost my exact same age. Our birthdays were only a few weeks apart. When she told me that, I turned to her.

"Do you think my parents hate me?" I asked.

I was good and drunk now. Not sloppy. But drunk enough to be showing all of my cards to this total stranger.

"I think, if you were *my* daughter," Stacy said. "I'd be so "goddamn" proud of you."

I shook my head, wondering if angels were allowed to say "goddamn" and hoping they were, because I really wanted what she said to be true. I really wanted her to be an angel.

I motioned to the bartender that I was ready to cash out and pulled out my phone to call an Uber. I'd find a way to come back and get my car sometime later.

"I got it," Stacy told me.

I would have protested. But then again, when an angel offers to buy your drinks, you don't argue. So I hugged her. Before I walked out the door, I turned around.

"You're an angel!" I said.

"You're drunk," she smiled back.

When I climbed in my Uber, my driver read the address I had typed into the app, which was the address of that little garden apartment.

"Actually," I said before he could get going. "Can you take me to the water?"

————————

I sat on the shore of the ocean, all alone but not feeling so alone anymore and running my fingers through the sand. The sun was setting and the night was soft, like cotton candy. I put my hand on my stomach, which didn't feel quite so empty anymore. There was something there. Some weight. Some substance to me.

I wondered about what Noah had said, about being desperate to be loved, and what Angel Stacy had said about being proud of me, and about a woman marrying a man who wants her about as much as she wants herself.

It occurred to me, slowly, that if this was the case, maybe my marriage hadn't been such a terrible failure after all. Because maybe JD had shown me something I couldn't have seen any other way. Maybe JD, in some insane and twisted way, had shown me myself.

I wanted it to be true, and I also didn't want it to be true—that he had shown me *me*. That we were the same in that way. Because if this were true, and I worried it was, then I had far more leverage than I ever realized. I could find my way out of this mess.

The only problem was I had no idea where to start.

# CHAPTER 10
# LOVE YOUR WAY OUT

---

*In the flush of love's light, we dare be brave*
*And suddenly we see that love costs all we are and will ever be.*
*Yet it is only love which sets us free.*

**—Maya Angelou**

At the end of every yoga practice, Sarah always says this thing about being in your life with your whole heart. She says it like a declaration, "I am in my life with my whole heart," and that has always struck me.

Part of me wonders if this is actually what it means to be *in love*—to be in our lives with our whole hearts. Maybe it has nothing to do with being a boyfriend or a girlfriend or a husband or a "good wife" and has everything to do with putting our whole weight into it, going all the way for what really matters to us.

In yoga, they say you're entitled to your effort, but not your outcomes. Maybe this is true with love, too. Maybe while we've been trying so hard to make love work, we forgot love was already working. Our job was only and ever to give ourselves over to it. Our whole hearts.

This makes sense to me. It's an offering.

If this is true, we never have to wonder what to do next or where to start. Where we start, always, is with one hand on our belly and one hand on our heart, and both feet on the floor. We give the only thing love has ever been able to give, and the only thing anyone can ever ask of us: the truth of where we are right now.

At times, I have to be honest, this doesn't seem like quite enough. Other times, it feels like more than anyone could possibly give. I think I'm starting to see how it's both.

---

On my last night in LA, I laid awake in bed listening to the sound of the crickets and the people passing by, the silence and the sound of my own thoughts. I was getting used to this by now. My time on the west coast was winding down, and I wondered what life was going to be like when I got home.

I pictured walking back into that house. I knew it would be different now. Things felt different. I felt different. And at the same time, I dreaded what I knew I would have to face when I got back there.

I fell asleep around midnight, and a few hours later I sat straight up in bed, startled.

I put my hands to my face and rubbed my eyes. I reached for my phone—2:10 a.m. What was I doing awake? That's when it happened. Like clarity dropped from the sky and into my brain, a list came to me.

What to do next:

*Sell your house*
*Sell your car*
*Change your name*
*Build your business*

*Get ready for the next thing*

I reached for my journal, which was on the nightstand, and flipped on the light. I needed to write this down, so I didn't forget any of it. I scribbled the list and then stared at what was in front of me. It felt good and right. Getting rid of the house, the Mercedes, and my married last name—that all felt like forward-movement. I wanted to move forward.

At the same time, I felt nervous. What if I did all of these things and everything fell apart?

I woke up the next morning with that journal still next to me in the bed, one hand gently resting on the cover.

After everything was packed, and I was ready to walk out the door of that garden apartment for good, I held my phone in my hand and slid the journal into my bag. Then, I whispered something to myself before I slipped out the door.

*God, please don't let me miss it.*

---

That prayer about "missing it" is something I prayed off and on through this whole process. Now, looking back, I wish I could whisper back to myself, to that younger version of me, *you cannot mess this up. Even if you tried. There's no such thing as missing it.*

I flew home and the first thing I did, after dropping my suitcase at the house, was go straight to the social security office. I figured in order to buy a new car, I needed an ID with my last name, and in order to do that, I needed to go through the name change process.

So I stood in line for nearly an hour and paid the fee and was handed a sheet of paper I could take to the DMV. Then I sat in traffic for forty-five minutes on my way across town. As I sat there in bumper-to-bumper traffic, that was the first time I started to doubt myself.

What was I doing? Was I wasting time? Changing my name could probably wait. But I took a few deep breaths and kept going.

I filled out all of my paperwork at the DMV and sat in the little seats they have for you until they called my name 90 minutes later. I tapped my foot anxiously in the waiting room the entire time, thinking about all the other more efficient things I could be doing.

When my name was called, I went to window eight and handed the woman there my paperwork.

"What brings you in?"

"A legal name change."

"Marriage or divorce?"

"Divorce."

The whole thing was very transactional, as you'd expect the DMV to be. That is until I said the word *divorce*.

"Congratulations," she smiled.

For a minute, this broke the tension. I laughed a little but told her divorce was miserable and that I wouldn't wish it on anyone. There was a pause. She stared directly at my paperwork but spoke again.

"I hear you. I've been there. Twice."

When she said that, I immediately softened. I thought of Angel Stacy. Divorced twice. I'm learning this now, that when a detail repeats itself in your life, to pay attention. Because sometimes—not always, but often—it's like a little whisper, telling you something. A secret.

I looked at the woman's name tag now, which said Nancy. Nancy shuffled papers and checked little boxes and reached for the credit card in my hand. I wanted to say something, but I couldn't think of anything even to say.

"I'm sorry," I finally managed.

"Don't be. It has taken me a long time to figure out who I have been all along."

I smiled. Suddenly, standing there at the DMV, it felt like I was supposed to be there. Right there. Right that minute. With Nancy.

I thought about how if anything had gone differently—the line at the social security office, or the traffic, or the woman who opened the door for me on the way into the DMV—I wouldn't have been there. I would have been standing at a different window, with a different person, who hadn't been divorced twice, and who never would have told me what Nancy just told me.

*It's taken me a long time to figure out who I've been all along.*

Standing there with Nancy at the DMV, I wondered if this was what it felt like to be in love. To be in your life with your whole heart. I smiled. Nancy was clear, like water. You could see right through her. And for the first time in a long time, I was feeling pretty clear, too.

---

On Monday morning, I woke early to go look at cars. It was now full-blown summer in Nashville, so stepping outside felt like climbing into a sauna with your clothes on. Getting in and out of cars and sitting on leather seats felt like a slip-and-slide. I texted friends, telling them I felt like I should be wearing a swimsuit.

I went to multiple dealerships. You know how it goes with car shopping. One dealership offers you a better trade-in value for your car. Another dealership offers you a better price on the vehicle. One dealership has the car you like better, even though it's out of your budget. And no matter where you go, you constantly feel like someone is about to take advantage of you and you're going to drive away with a lemon.

By the end of the first day of shopping, I was exhausted and frustrated, and the only car I found that seemed worth buying was one on the west side of town which was nice, but really more money than I had been planning to spend, and I couldn't decide what to do.

I considered selling the car privately on Craigslist, but the thought of meeting strangers in parking lots and negotiating a price for a product I could not possibly know less about seemed like torture to me. So instead, I bought a bottle of wine and box of ice cream bars and went home to decide what to do next.

There, in the quiet of my house and all alone, I whispered again.

*God, please don't let me miss it.*

---

"Sarah, what do you mean when you say *I'm in my life with my whole heart?*" I asked her the next time we met at the yoga studio.

"I can show you better than I can tell you," she said.

"Ok, will you?"

Sarah got right to work. She had me do planks and hold them for three minutes. Just when I thought I was about to die, she'd have me flip onto my right arm, or my left arm, and hold the side plank for another 60 seconds.

Then, jumping jacks. This hardly felt like yoga to me. But she had me stand up straight, reach for my feet, jump back to a plank pose, lift myself back to a forward fold and then stand up again. Like yoga burpees. Each time I stood up, she'd have me make a loud noise.

"Huh!" She coached me.

"Huh!" I tried.

"Louder!" she screamed.

Then she had me lay flat on my back and put my legs up to the sky, so that they made a ninety degree angle. I knew what this meant. I'd done this with her before. With my toes pointed up to the sky, I criss-crossed my feet, back and forth, back and forth. But now, instead of moving slowly, she had me do this faster and faster and faster.

She turned music on and turned the volume up so you could really feel the vibrations in the floor.

"We're going to do this for three minutes," Sarah said, clapping her hands together.

"Even faster!" She yelled.

"Sarah!"

"Three minutes—you can do this!" she shouted back.

When it was all over, I collapsed to the floor, my whole body shaking. Sweat was rolling off of my face and dripping onto the mat in front of me. My heart was racing in my chest.

"Was that it?" I asked.

"No, *this* is it, Ally," she pointed at me. "We're much better able to discern the truth when we're in our bodies."

"I'm shaking," I said.

"Trembling is how we know we are in a relationship," Sarah said, smiling.

---

When you make a decision to change your life, you expect things will get better right away. After all—you're finally doing things differently. The outcome should be different, right? But one thing I'm learning is things often actually get worse before they get better. They get harder. More tense. More challenging.

Julia Cameron says this is like a space shuttle leaving the atmosphere. The resistance we feel should be expected. It's the resistance of leaving one world and moving into a new one.

I made a decision about the car. I was going to go back to the west side of town and get the car I liked, but was a little bit out of my budget. On the one hand, this seemed like the *worst* possible decision I could make, the thing I had been taught never to do—to spend a bunch of money on a car. And at the same time, this seemed like the best decision I knew how to make. I was trying. Taking my best stab at being in my life with my whole heart. I would find a way to make it work.

I climbed in the Mercedes, feeling the pressure. Looking back now, I can see what a *small* deal this was, buying a car. But back then, on that day, I kept wondering what was going to happen if I screwed this all up.

I typed the name of the dealership into my GPS, hit "start" and then called my friend Gina to tell her what I was doing, to see if she would talk me out of it.

On the phone, I told Gina the whole story and asked her what she thought I should do.

"I think you should trust yourself."

She reminded me that I didn't have to do anything I didn't want to do, and that this was a decision I got to make, on my own. She told me I could go to the dealership and test drive the car again, and ask whatever questions I wanted, and that even at the last minute if I needed to change my mind, that was ok. She told me I didn't owe those car salesman anything.

"You can trust yourself, Ally. You can."

The line was silent for a minute. As I made the next turn, I looked down at my GPS and realized it was taking me the wrong direction. I double-checked the destination. It said the name of the dealership. Maybe there was a second location?

*Oh well,* I figured. *I might as well go see if there's anything I like on their other lot.*

Gina asked if I could bring myself to believe that maybe—perhaps—I could show up exactly as myself in the world and that everything would turn out just great.

"You mean with my whole heart?" I asked.

"Yes, I guess with your whole heart." Gina said.

I hung up the phone with Gina and walked inside. The first person I met was David.

---

When the door swung open to the dealership, a man walked across the floor to greet me.

"Hi, I'm David," he said. "How can I help?"

I pointed to the Mercedes outside and told him I was looking for something I could trade pretty evenly.

"I was driving to your other location to buy a car I drove the other day, but I ended up here by accident."

"Let me show you what we have on the lot."

We walked across the lot, and he showed me a few cars that would be in my price range. I test drove two or three of them and then came back to sit at David's desk. I was still feeling so uncertain.

"What should I do?" I asked.

"I can't tell you what to do," he said, smiling.

"What would you do if you were me?"

I know it's just a car, but you'll see later why what he said next mattered so much to me.

"Honestly, if I were you," he said. "I would not buy a car today. I would take a few months. I would keep looking. I'll stay in touch and let you know if we get any trade-ins that look like they might work for you."

I was silent.

"I know that's not what you want to hear," he said.

"I… I… appreciate your honesty," I stuttered.

I thought back to what Gina had said. Maybe I could show up as myself, and I would be safe and supported in the world. Maybe it really was enough—to be in this life with my whole heart.

I shook David's hand, left the dealership and went to Whole Foods down the street. I bought sushi and a kombucha and checked my email. Then, out of nowhere, something came over me. It was the same feeling I'd gotten with the to-do list. It went like this.

*Go back.*

*Go back? Are you joking me? What was I going to do if I went back? He'll think I'm completely nuts*, I told myself. And maybe I was. Still, I could not overcome the urge I had to go back to the dealership—that if I was going to buy a car, it was going to be from David.

Laughing to myself a little, I got up from my seat, threw my garbage away in the very complicated receptacles, gathered my things, and climbed into that Mercedes. I mean, what did I have to lose?

I pulled into the driveway of the dealership and walked in the door. David was standing right there. That was the first time I really noticed how handsome he was.

"What are you doing here? he asked.

"Look," I said, "I just went through a divorce and that car belonged to my ex-husband. I can't drive it anymore. I need you to help me find a new one."

A look of understanding came over his face when I said that, and suddenly I felt like I knew what he was about to say.

"I understand," He said. "I've been there. Twice."

And there it was again—like a tidal wave of healing and grace and understanding—feeling like there was no way I was standing here by accident. I thought of Angel Stacy and of Nancy.

We both stood there for a few seconds, smiling.

"Forget that dirt bag" he said, finally. "Let's get you a new car."

---

We sat at David's desk for another 30 minutes that day, looking on the computer for another car that would work for me. I found one I liked, but it needed to have some work done, so he told me he would look into it and be in touch. We stayed in contact that week, texting and talking on the phone, mostly about cars, but eventually not so much about cars.

At one point, I asked him if he would ever be interested in meeting me for a drink.

I shocked myself completely when I did that—partly because I had this whole idea that I was going to wait a year after my divorce was final to date anyone, and partly because I was asking *him* on a date, and partly because I was not at all unaware of how truly strange and probably inappropriate it was to ask out your car salesman. Still, I couldn't help myself.

This was it. The truth of who I was in the moment. Me being in my life with my whole heart.

I heard somewhere once that you can either be in love or you can be in control, but not both. I have not stopped thinking about that since, about how much time I have spent being in control and about how good it feels to be in love. It's the gentlest grief, letting go of who we thought we were supposed to be. It has taken me a long time to figure out who I have been all along.

---

I met David at a place called Old Glory—a little speakeasy-style bar hidden in the back of Edgehill Village in Nashville. It was particularly hot that day, and I hadn't eaten much, which wasn't a great combination. But I wore a black sundress I had picked out from my friend Vanessa's closet, and as I walked out the door of my house, I caught a glimpse of my reflection in the mirror. It was the first time in ages I hadn't cringed looking at myself.

My eyes weren't so sunken anymore, and my skin was looking brighter and softer these days. I looked like myself. For the first time in ages, I thought I maybe even looked a little bit pretty.

I arrived first and found us a table—one tucked in the back of the restaurant. My hands were shaking and sweaty. But David arrived a few minutes later, and we settled into an easy conversation.

"There's something I should get out of the way right now," David said, not five minutes into our conversation. "In case you wanted to run for the door."

I laughed nervously.

"I've been divorced twice. You know this. I sell cars—this is not news to you either. But you should also know I have four children. The youngest is four. The oldest is nineteen."

He looked at me.

It's funny because for whatever reason, in that moment, any anxiety I had been feeling melted. I shook my head, thinking about how much time I had spent figuring out the "right" thing to do when there was something so calming about this—someone who was right here, right now, right where he was, telling the truth and in his life with his whole heart.

"You don't have to stay," David said.

I shook my head and smiled.

"Let's get something to eat."

David asked me pointed questions like I'd never been asked on a first date. Like why I had gotten divorced. I didn't feel grilled or unsettled about answering them. It felt good and soft to be sitting here with him. I could feel his kindness. I could also feel the two glasses of whiskey. So I told him everything. The whole story.

When I finished, David looked at me and then back down at his cocktail and then back at me. Then he said something I was not expecting.

"I bet that guy really regrets losing you."

I was so taken aback by this response. I expected him to say he would *never* do anything like that to a woman, or to threaten to punch JD if he ever saw him in a bar someday. But as I sat there at the table looking across at him, I realized how what he was saying instead was actually somehow better. I didn't quite understand it then—which is why I'm sure it's still fuzzy to you now. I'll have to tell you more later.

For now, know that as we sat there sipping our cocktails and smiling, the sensation that came over me was that everything was happening right on time. On purpose. It was the sense that I needed to be here, right now, with this person. And that as little sense as it made right then, that was ok. I was in my life with my whole heart.

Have you ever thought about how many things have to go exactly, perfectly right for you to end up right where you are right now? Have you ever considered that even the things that have gone "wrong" in your life have had to go just perfectly *as they went* so you could be right here—wherever that is? It baffles me when I think about it, when I look back. It baffles me when I look forward, trying to know things I can't possibly know.

It's good we don't know everything ahead of time, I think. I am learning to enjoy the suspense.

––––––––––

David walked me to my car, which was parked on the street right outside of Old Glory. But as we stood there, saying goodbye, and he opened my driver's side door for me, I realized there was no un-embarrassing way to do this.

My plan had been to let him walk away and then call an Uber. But now that he was standing there waiting for me, I realized I was going to have to tell him.

"I don't think I can drive home," I said, smiling.

David offered to buy my car an overnight pass and move it to the lot, so I wouldn't get towed.

"Let me give you a ride home. Are you ok with that?"

He opened his car door to let me in and then climbed into the driver's side. And when we were both sitting there, I did the weirdest thing. I did not mean to do it. It didn't make any sense. But I reached my hand across the center console and grabbed his. I could feel his heartbeat in his palm. So soft. I wondered if he could feel mine.

"Where am I taking you?" David asked.

"Can we take the long way home?"

# CHAPTER 11

# THE SECRET BEAUTY OF YOU

---

*"Since only love is real, only the love you were given and that which you gave others, was real in your past. Nothing else need be brought with you into the shining present. Leave behind what wasn't real to begin with, and every moment can be a new beginning."*
**—Marianne Williamson**

The thing you're supposed to do if you get caught in a riptide, they say, is to surrender. You're not supposed to fight it. If you fight it, it will kill you. But if you can bring yourself to soften— to give yourself over to the thing— eventually it will pull you all the way around, and all the way back to the surface of the water again.

It's crazy to think about the logic of this, how fighting against the riptide is the surest way to drown, even though it is the only thing that makes any logical sense. How could the one thing that *saves* you be the thing that makes the least practical sense?

I haven't wanted to do this—to give myself over to something when I had no idea how things were going to end up. I haven't trusted myself enough. I haven't trusted love enough. Not until now.

———————

We were on our fourth date when David invited me to go to the ocean with him. He said it under his breath, to the point where I thought I may have misheard him. I asked him what he was doing for the fourth of July, and he mentioned he was going to Seaside, Florida—a small town about an 8-hour drive from Nashville.

His kids were on vacation with their mom and stepdad, so he was taking the trip by himself.

"What are you doing for the weekend?" he asked.

"No plans."

That's when it happened, the thing I was not expecting, but that stirred something inside of me like a riptide, a furious under-the-water current.

"Do you want to come?"

Again, his voice was quiet when he said it, and it was also right before taking a big bite of his cheeseburger.

"Did you just ask me if I want to come with you?" I waited.

He smiled.

And for the rest of the night, neither of us said another word about it.

It had been a week since our date at Old Glory. We left that night and drove through the city, taking the long way as I had requested. We drove from Edgehill, down Music Row, and then over to West Nashville, Radnor Park, driving and talking and listening to music.

"What about this song?" I said, playing a country top 40 hit song I was sure he would hate. He looked at me, smiled, and then reached over to turn the volume up.

He walked me to my doorstep that night. He actually stood there while I turned the key and opened the front door, and then waited for me to go in. I said goodbye. Before he turned around, he smiled.

"You're beautiful," he said.

Then, quickly, he turned his back to me and I peered around the corner until he disappeared into his car. I could not stop smiling.

The next morning, David sent a message early to see if I had a plan for getting my car. I responded and told him I was planning to call an Uber in just a few minutes.

He texted back. *Will you let me take you? Coffee included.*

We went to Eighth and Roast, one of my favorites. The place was packed on a Saturday morning, so instead of staying to sit, we took our drinks with us and got in his car. We drove through the hills of Tennessee.

"How did you get started selling cars?" I asked.

"You mean my *dream job*?"

"I mean you don't strike me as a typical car salesman. I tried to buy a car from you and you told me to get lost," I laughed.

"Well, when my ex-wife left me in Birmingham, she came to Tennessee with my kids, and I couldn't bear the thought of not being near them. So I made plans to move, but I had signed a non-compete in my industry back in Alabama. And I had a friend who worked in the car business in Tennessee, so…"

I nodded.

"So here I am," he said.

"Well. I'm glad you're here."

A few days later we met at a juice bar. We drank green juice and sat across the table, and I asked him what he missed most about his old life, in Alabama.

"Coming home to my kids," he said without hesitating.

I pictured David walking in the door of his house in Alabama and his kids running to meet him at the door.

"Sometimes you don't know what you have until it's gone, Ally. I've made a lot of mistakes in my life. I'm not who you think I am."

"You're a good dad, David."

"If I were a good dad, I would be there when my kid got home from school to teach him to play catch."

"Hey, bad dads don't sit around thinking about how they could come home from work earlier so they could play catch with their kids."

David changed the subject.

"Tell me something. What on earth made you decide to get married in four months?"

"Ha! You're really turning this back around on me, aren't you?"

I thought about it for a long minute.

"You know, I told him once I wanted to wait?"

"You did?"

"Yeah. Actually, twice while we were engaged. I asked if maybe we could have a little more time."

"And?"

"He told me I was just scared, and that it was ok to be scared, but that I shouldn't let fear drive my actions."

"Wow."

"Yeah. Then, right before we separated—at one of our very last appointments with the therapist together—I told him that if I could go back and do anything differently, if I could just do one thing differently, I would have put my foot down about that. I would have said I wasn't getting married to him unless we waited."

"And?"

"He told me he wouldn't have waited."

David leaned back in his chair like he was feeling really uncomfortable. He stretched his hands to the ceiling, and when he leaned forward again, he said something I could have never known I needed to hear. He said it quietly, leaning across the table.

"He loved you, Ally. I feel like you should know that. He loved you, but he was the one who was scared. He was doing the best he could."

"The best he could?"

"I'm not saying you should go back to the guy. No. It's so good you got out. I'm just saying he loved you and, yes, he was doing the best he could. Sometimes our best just really, really sucks."

I thought about that. I wasn't sure.

The memory of the juice bar faded, and now I was back in the burger joint with David, where he had just asked me to go to the ocean with him. The sun was setting and white lights were strung over our head, and everything was turning pink and thick like bubble gum.

David asked for our check.

There were so many things I wanted to tell him, but none of it made any sense. I wanted to tell him I was feeling something for him that I couldn't explain but that felt good, and I didn't want it to end. I wanted to say he was helping me to forgive JD, and to forgive myself. I wanted to tell him that I thought we were *supposed* to be here, together, in some strange way—that none of this was an accident. I wanted to ask him if he would ask me to go to the ocean with him again.

But I couldn't bring myself to say any of it. So instead, I just sighed deeply.

"Let me take you home," David said.

―――――――――

The next day David called while I was sitting on the floor of my bedroom. He was driving to the beach.

"I know last night I mentioned you coming to the beach, but it probably sounded like I was joking. I wasn't joking. If you want to come, I'd really love to buy you a ticket."

I wasn't sure what to say.

"There's no expectation," David went on, answering my questions before I even asked them. "You'll have your own bedroom, and there are no strings attached. I just thought you might be able to get some writing done. You don't even have to spend any time with me if you don't want."

I laughed.

I wanted to say yes. I really did. And at the same time, I wasn't sure I could do it.

"Can I have some time to think about it?"

"Take all the time you need," he said.

I hung up the phone and leaned my head on the wall where I was sitting and thought about what to do. What did I want to do? The thing is, and I'm finally just now starting to get better at noticing this, I knew exactly what I wanted to do. I just wasn't sure I was strong enough to do it quite yet. I'm getting there.

---

The next morning I met my friend Kate for a hike around Radnor Lake. We wandered through the woods right at sunrise, plodding through the soft trail, and I told her about David for the first time.

This might sound strange, but I had been avoiding telling people about him. I worried they would judge me for dating so close to my divorce, worried they would judge David for being divorced twice, worried someone would try to talk me out of having my process.

"We've been out five times, Kate, and he hasn't even tried to kiss me," I told her.

"Forget the divorces—there's the strike against him!" Kate joked.

We laughed and kept walking. I also told Kate about him inviting me to the beach.

"And?"

"The idea of being at the beach with him is… perfect." I said. "Everything about it. Everything in me is telling me to go."

"So why not go?"

It took me a couple of minutes to think about it. Nothing that came to mind felt quite right. Then, all of a sudden, I knew.

"I'm going to ruin it, Kate. I always ruin it."

I surprised myself with the words coming out of my mouth, because by now, even I knew they weren't true. But it's amazing how long these thought patterns live in your body—in your cells—long after you've banished them from your mind.

It takes a *long* time to figure out who you've been all along.

Kate sighed.

"You've been through a lot, Ally. And you're still standing here, you're still showing up in your life everyday. You are doing it. You are doing such a good job. You can trust yourself."

"I want to go."

"Then go!"

"I don't think I can let him buy me a plane ticket. It's too expensive. It's too much."

"You know. It's only a 7 hour drive…"

I smiled.

The next morning I woke up at 5 a.m. and drove from Nashville to Seaside, Florida. I felt a bit trembly as I drove, softer and more vulnerable than I had felt in a long time. As the sun came up over the highway, it felt like something big and important was coming.

I was right, and also wrong—and so many things I didn't even know just yet.

———

At the beach, we rented paddle boards. We walked to the bright yellow building across the street where there was a sign that said it so big you couldn't miss it. *BIKES, SURF BOARDS, PADDLE BOARDS.*

It took some finagling, since paddle boards are not small, but we picked out two of them and managed to get them across the street and out to the beach.

We spent hours out on the water that morning and afternoon, under the sun, trying to stand up and falling in the water and giggling at how much harder this was than it looked. By the end, David and I were sun-soaked and sandy and salty, and we both lay on our backs, letting the water take us wherever it wanted to go.

At one point, I rolled over onto my stomach and propped myself up on my elbows.

"It's peaceful out here, isn't it?" I said, letting the water buoy me back and forth, back and forth.

I scanned the beach for where our chairs were. They were far enough away from us now that they were looking pretty tiny. I cupped my hand over my eyes, squinting to see if I could still see them.

David saw me looking and laughed.

"Just think, we're going to have to paddle all the way back there."

I rolled over again and let the water carry me, let it take us down the shore. But I couldn't help but think about how amazing it was that the ocean was this powerful, that the tides were this powerful, they could carry us this easily.

I thought about what Sarah always said about grace—what she had told me that day about about how the first part was enduring the unendurable, and now it was time for the second part. This felt like the second part. A great opening. Total surrender.

"What do you want to do tonight?" David asked.

"This," I said without thinking.

"Ha. You want to lay on these paddle boards all night?"

I giggled.

I propped myself up on my side, turning to face him, my arm cupping my head. It was beautiful out here. I loved this feeling, all free and safe and soft and happy and warm.

"David, I don't ever want it to end."

---

We made it back to the condo at right about sunset. The sky was doing its incredible thing, turning all those amazing colors and dancing for us. So without doing anything, without showers or make-up or even changing out of our swimsuits, we sat out on the back deck of the condo and watched it happen together. Like spectators at an orchestra performance or something. We hardly said a thing the entire time.

I let it happen. What other choice do we really have?

At one point, I looked over at David and thought about how perfect he looked in that light. So like himself. That was the phrase that came to mind. A photographer friend told me once this is called golden hour, the time of day when the light is just exactly right. It's fleeting. It only lasts for a little bit. But while it lasts, everything looks flawless. Part of me has to wonder if this is how we're *supposed* to look. If this is how we actually look—all of us—the way we looked as the sun was setting that night.

Sitting there on the porch, I admired David, secretly. He was perfect, actually. Both of us were. We couldn't be any more beautiful if we tried.

---

We left the condo right after the sun went down to dinner. David had made reservations for us.

The hostess escorted us to our seats, and I loved the way David asked the waiter his name, right from the very beginning of the meal. I loved the way he asked questions about the menu, and I loved the way he would finally say, after asking a half a dozen questions about the appetizers, "we want one of everything!"

"There's still a lot we don't know about each other," David said, after our server walked away.

"That is true. What do you want to know?"

He paused for a minute before speaking again.

"How do you feel about electric can openers?"

"I hate them."

"That's it," David said. "You're perfect for me."

We both laughed.

After dinner, we walked down the street where the fireworks show was taking place and sat on a ledge, surrounded by crowds of people. I was feeling cocooned with David, though, like we were all alone. We watched the fireworks, and I leaned into the crook of his arm. That was when I noticed how, for the first time in a long time, I was letting my guard down.

"Are you going to kiss me?" I asked him.

"Ally," he shook his head. "I'm no good for you. I'm a mess. I'm not who you think I am."

I looked away. Suddenly I felt like maybe I shouldn't have come here, like I had gotten this all wrong again. If he was really a mess, I was going to get hurt all over again. And if he *was* a mess, then why did I feel so like myself with him?

I tossed and turned that night, all tangled up and feeling like nothing had changed. I was still the same person I had always been. All the way back to the beginning. As if I had made no progress. *Oh God, how do I keep missing it?*

―――――――――

The next morning I woke early and wandered down to the ocean, just as the sun was rising. The water was warm, so I got all the way in. I let myself float. I let the water carry me. I stayed there for the longest time thinking about what it felt like to sink into the ease of something.

An hour later, I made my way back up to the condo. I found David in the kitchen.

"I have to go."

"Home?"

"Yeah, back to Nashville."

"Don't go," he said. I could tell he was feeling badly, like he was the reason I was leaving. But the truth was, he wasn't. I was the reason I was leaving.

"I have to get my house on the market. It's a to-do list thing..." I trailed off. It was hard to explain.

David told me he understood. I went to take a shower and pack my things. While I was getting ready, I heard him leave the condo. When he returned, I was ready to go and he was standing in the kitchen with two coffee cups. He handed me one of them.

"I filled your car with gas," David said, handing me the keys.

I searched his face but he wouldn't look at me, so I didn't say anything else. We grabbed my luggage and walked down to the car, where he loaded everything into the trunk for me.

We stood at my driver's side door for a minute. When I hugged him goodbye, I thanked him for everything and then said one more thing before I climbed in.

"You aren't a mess, David."

I drove down the road wondering what would happen next. Oh, how I wished we could know what happens next. When I was ten minutes away, I pulled down the visor to block the sun and something fell into my lap. It was a plain white piece of paper. I held it up so I could read it.

*I should have kissed you*, it said.

I smiled and laughed to myself and couldn't stop thinking about how good it is that we don't know, how easy it always feels to ride the current—to let love take us all the way home.

---

I came home from the beach feeling ready to write for the first time in months. That surprised me since it seemed to come out of nowhere, but I did not resist it. I let it happen. All the way.

I walked in the front door and dumped my bags in the front hallway of my house. Contractors were coming to the house in the morning to do some painting so I could put it on the market, but I wasn't thinking about any of that. Instead, I went straight for the cabinet in the living room where I stored my Sharpies and 3x5 cards.

I dumped everything out on the floor.

I started with stories, making up the process as I went along. I wrote things on those cards like "gatorade" and "car shopping" and "wedding day" and "Mikey." I wrote, "telling Sarah" and "driving to Betsy's house" and "finding yoga." Once I had a mass of cards, I started arranging them in order on the ground all around me.

I didn't know what I was doing, and yet somehow, I did.

I sat in that mess of cards and Sharpies and paper and pens for *hours* with my hair all salty and wild and still in my beach clothes. I felt my way through the entire thing, until each of those stories were arranged as chapters, with all the details under them I knew I needed to include. By the time the sun went down, I had a book outlined.

I smiled at the sticky notes and post-it notes and 3x5 cards taped up all over my wall. For two years, I had been struggling to make this happen, had been trying to muscle it into place, had been trying to control and force and make it all make sense. Then for some reason today, it *happened*. It was all happening. Love was happening.

I laid in bed that night and closed my eyes, and I could still hear the sound of the waves. In and out, in and out. I could still feel what it felt like to float in the water that morning. It was so easy. Just so terribly, impossibly easy I could hardly believe I had waited this long to do it.

# CHAPTER 12
## SWEET RELEASE

---

*"Some say love is a burning thing,*
*That it makes a fiery ring*
*Oh but I know love as a caging thing*
*Just a killer, come to call from some awful dream…"*
—**Matthew Houck** (Phosphorescent)

I find quite a bit of solace in the fact that the hero of the story doesn't know she's the hero. Notoriously, I'm told, heroes in stories feel inadequate and under-prepared and ill-equipped and out of place. The hero worries she's making the wrong decisions. She makes the wrong decisions. She walks down fateful paths—even while the audience screams, "Don't do it!". She cannot seem to get it right.

But this doesn't change the fact that she *is* the hero. The only one responsible for her own destiny, the only one who can possibly rescue herself from her own pain.

She is the one we're all watching, with admiration.

Once my house was on the market, I started looking for a new place to live. I drove around town and looked at dozens of apartments—all of which seemed too loud, or too overpriced, or too smells-like-macaroni-and-cheese-in-the-hallway. Finally one afternoon, when I was supposed to be working on another work project, I pulled up Craigslist and there, the very first posting, bright and shining, was my perfect apartment.

It had all the things I wanted. High ceilings. Bright white fixtures. Wood floors. A back deck, which looked out over a pond. Without pausing for even a second to think, I sent an email. *Can I come see it in person?*

Just like that, we made an appointment.

As I drove, I knew this was my place. I was getting used to this now—this feeling of trusting myself, of really going with the flow on things, of riding the momentum. It was exhilarating at points. Devastating at others, but I hadn't gotten there quite yet.

I met the owner at the front door, and he walked me through condo, which was even more beautiful in person than it had been in the pictures.

"Were you just sitting on Craigslist, hitting refresh every couple of minutes?" he asked, as I opened each of the cabinet doors, trying to act like I wasn't too eager.

I laughed a little.

"Why, fast response?"

"Record-setting."

"I'm just… I'm ready for a new season," I said, smiling.

We walked out onto the back deck, which faced out over a small pond.

"The sun sets right over there," the owner said, pointing into the distance. "It comes down right behind that steeple. I bought this place weeks before I met my wife and we used to love sitting out here, drinking wine, staring at the hills."

I put both of my hands on the railing. Honestly, it was probably too big for just me. I didn't need this much space. And I was sure I could find something cheaper, so that I wouldn't have to worry so much about making money and could focus on my writing.

But I thought about how nice it would be not to have to get rid of all of the furniture from the house—I could keep everything—and about what the owner had just said about buying this place right before he met his wife. The whole thing felt symbolic to me. Symbolic of a life that was not in shambles, the way I still worried mine was.

Here I was, four months past my divorce, and for a brief moment while I was standing there, it felt like maybe the nightmare could be over. The pain could be over. The heartbreak could be over. It felt like this small reassurance that life after divorce could be even more beautiful than I ever thought.

I have learned, by now, to be skeptical of all-or-nothing, total transformation, overnight-everything-is-different kind of thinking. I have learned how truly rare it is for stories to unfold like that. It's not that overnight change is impossible. It's just that most things, the kinds of things we want the most, happen slowly. Hearts heal slowly. Love grows slowly. Trees grow slowly. It's weeds that grow fast.

As I sat there on that back deck, dreaming about my unfolding relationship with David, and getting way ahead of myself, I wasn't thinking about any of that. I just closed my eyes and took a deep breath and did what heroes do in their stories. What they *have* to do. Their only choice. I made the best decision I knew how with the information I had. What a brilliant, beautiful thing it was to do.

I'm so "goddamn" proud of myself.

"I'll take it," I said.

———

David came home from the beach, and I took him to see the new place I had found. I showed him everything—pointing out the ceilings and the floors and the back deck with the sunsets.

"Oh Ally, I love it," he told me.

"You haven't even seen the best part yet," I told him, grabbing his hand, leading him around to the back, where the water was. We crossed a small footbridge and walked over to the back of the building. I told him what the owner had said about meeting his wife right after he bought this place.

"Apparently they would sit out on the back deck every night and drink wine."

I didn't tell David it was *him* I dreamed of sitting with on that back deck, drinking wine. Maybe he knew. I still don't know. But that night, he looked at me and smiled.

It was right about sunset, so the sky was glowing pink and purple and orange and yellow and we stood there, at the edge of the water, watching the sun dip down behind the hills, watching the light dance over the surface of the pond. It was golden hour again.

David pulled me close and kissed me for the first time.

"Perfect, right?" I asked when I pulled away.

He looked at me.

"Perfect."

That night, I let love happen. All the way. It wasn't something I had planned to do. In fact, I surprised myself completely when I invited David up to my room, and then again, when he hesitated, and I asked again. This was unlike me, this thing I was doing. It was not the formula I had been taught. It was not the formula I had followed for so long.

But it was honest and true and where I was at right in that moment, and it was me being in my life with my whole heart. It was one of the more spectacular things I have ever done.

In the weeks following, I felt like someone had taken the lid off of me. I did not have to coax myself out of bed in the morning anymore, and I didn't sit staring at a blank page any longer when it came time to do my writing. In fact, this book was pouring out of me, faster than anything I had ever written.

I felt like I was on fire. I felt like I had come up from underwater and could breathe again.

I sent chapters to my agent, but he didn't like them. They weren't what we had talked about, he told me, and I felt myself getting furious on the phone. Just completely furious. Of *course* they weren't what we had talked about. I was a completely different person now than I was when we had first talked about them.

I wondered, on certain days, what I was going to do without an agent who believed in this book. Or, anyone who believed in this book. But then I would wake up the next morning and do it again, putting one foot in front of the other.

A few words on the page every day. One step at a time.

I put off other work I felt like I should be doing to make money. I wondered at times if it would be worth it, or if I would put in all of this work, and the thing would sit on my computer forever. Then again, it occurred to me, the most important person who could ever believe in this book, already believed in it: me.

What a strange feeling it was to have myself back like that. That fiery, passionate, back-and-forth, up-and-down woman I was. What a strange and petrifying feeling to be back in my own body, to be in my life with my whole heart.

———————

I should have seen what came next, but I did not. I should have seen it because I was doing this very familiar thing again—making my story all about someone other than me, handing over the keys to my life. Love is way too kind to let us do this to ourselves. Love will not let us miss it.

I told David one night, as we were laying in bed, that I didn't think I could live without him. That if he left, it would be worse than losing my marriage. I wasn't sure I would survive. I backpedaled after saying that, seeing the look on his face and realizing how terrible a thing it was to say, but the truth was already out.

A few nights later, I met him for a concert. We laughed and played and talked like everything was normal. But on the way back to my house, he told me I was fascinating, and I picked a fight with him about it. By fascinating, did he mean complicated and confusing? He told me that was *not* what he had said, but I argued with him.

When we got to my house, he told me he thought it would be better if he didn't come inside.

When he said that, the most crippling feeling came over me. It was an out-of-body experience. The last time I had felt this way was on the hotel bathroom back in Atlanta—when I thought there was a baby and there was no baby. I felt like such a fool.

"I am such an idiot," I whispered.

David told me he wasn't going anywhere, that he was going to take the night off and call me in the morning. But I didn't believe him. When I opened my mouth, I acted like a kid. I went all the way back to the beginning.

"Don't bother calling again," I said.

In that moment, I suddenly realized why people do it. Why they live their whole lives following the formula but disconnected from their hearts. Because now that I wasn't numb anymore, I was feeling everything—all the pain and all the fear I had been putting off for so long. It was unbearable. It was awful. It was the most terrifying thing I had ever felt.

Was this what it was like to be in my life with my whole heart? Was this what it took to be in love? Forget all of it. I wasn't strong enough. I didn't want to do it.

I went in my house and sat at the bottom of my stairs because I could not go up them—could not walk up to that room again, alone. I shook and I sobbed for a long, long time. I leaned my head against the wall. This was over. Love was a nightmare. I was a lost cause.

---

In a yoga class one time, someone stopped Sarah partway through the practice to tell her that she was just a beginner, meaning that the things Sarah was asking her to do were too hard for her. She wanted something easier. And I'll never forget what Sarah did next, because she stopped the entire class—a whole room of 40 people.

"Who of us are beginners?" she asked.

Every single hand in the room went up.

This is the thing I love most about love, I think. In love, we are reminded of our beginner selves, which are always with us. The parts of us we have done such a good job of covering and hiding and pretending don't exist. The childish parts. The resentful parts. The angry parts. The bitter parts. The unloved parts. The messy parts. The addicted parts. The parts that are so desperate for healing and attention. Love uncovers us. It teaches us how to be in our lives with our whole hearts.

In this way, love is what saves us. It is what heals us. Even the love that is messy or disappointing or infuriating or unfair. I mean, have you had a love that was any other way? Have you had a love that was perfectly trimmed around the edges? If you have, will you please tell us your secret? Where do you get the good drugs?

And for a long time, I thought the point of love was to make it last. To get it to work. To do all the moves. But the longer I do it, the more I realize love is having its way with us, those of us who will let it. Those of us who will let ourselves struggle like the beginners we are. Those of us who aren't afraid to get up and try again.

———————

The next morning, I felt furious with myself for what I had done. I couldn't believe it. Had nothing changed? Had I gone all the way back to the beginning?

At the same time, a small part of me thought, sure, I had picked a fight and I had acted immature. I had said something I didn't mean. But I hadn't been belittled or yelled at or felt forced to run from the car without shoes on. I got rejected. And I was alive. Things had changed. Not everything. But this was my offering. This was enough.

It takes a long time for change to sink all the way into our bodies. It takes years for change to become cellular, second nature. I have to remind myself of this—that I'm allowed to have my process, that I don't have to have it figured out all right this minute, that this is the whole point. Showing up. Being in my life with my whole heart.

I am a woman in love.

I called and texted and tried to apologize to David. For days I did this. And then weeks. I was sorry, and I wanted a second chance to stay with my breath and stay with him. I wanted to try again.

But there was no response.

# CHAPTER 13
# SHE IS ON FIRE

---

*"Until your knees finally hit the floor, you're just playing at life, and on some level you're scared because you know you're just playing. The moment of surrender is not when life is over. It's when it begins."*

**—Marianne Williamson**

Two weeks after David and I fell out of touch, there was a full moon, and I was falling completely apart. Sometimes you *think* you've fallen completely apart, and then something happens and you realize—no—there is still more unraveling to do.

It is easy to resent this part of the process—to think this is a sure-fire sign you've gone the wrong direction. But I am learning to see the cracking and melting and softening as a necessary part of the process. It *feels* like hell, but without it, you would never get to what is underneath—the love you've been running from all this time.

---

I woke early and dressed and looked at myself in the bathroom mirror that Sunday morning. I looked awful, honestly. Truly terrible. I hadn't looked this bad in months. I had been drinking too much and waking in the middle of the night, sweating and swimming in this puddle of myself.

I did my best to cover the dark circles with make-up and put on a pair of heels and nice shirt and walked out the door to meet my friends for brunch.

We met at a little cafe near my house called Margot—MJ and my friends Tracie, Emily, and Lindsley. We filtered in, and everyone hugged and started catching up. The girls ordered coffee, and I ordered a mimosa.

I think it was MJ who noticed first.

"You ok, Ally?"

All eyes turned my direction.

I opened my mouth but nothing came out. Instead, tears pressed against the back of my eyelids and heat ran through my body, like fire. I shook my head and everyone waited.

Time passed slowly. It's funny how grief does that—slows down time. Suddenly this thing that used to be the scarcest of all resources, this thing you never had enough of, this thing you were always racing against… now you're swimming in pools of it.

"Take a deep breath," MJ said, who noticed I had quit breathing.

"Everything has fallen apart," I said.

"What do you mean?"

"Everything is gone."

I thought about calling the owner of that apartment with the back deck and the sunsets and telling him I wouldn't be able to move in, after all. Tracie put her hand on my shoulder.

"I have these friends," I said. "They got caught in that terrible tornado in Joplin a few years ago. Do you remember?"

Everyone nodded.

"Eric was at work, and his wife, who'd just had a baby, was at home when the sirens first sounded. They were texting back and forth with each other, but they weren't too worried. This happened all the time. At one point, Torrie decided to go down to the storm cellar anyway—just to be safe. So she climbed down, and sat there, nursing the baby while the storm happened upstairs."

"Slowly, the thing became more and more violent, until Torrie could hear things breaking and shattering. That was when she started to feel like this might be worse than she had imagined. Slowly, the floor where she was sitting started to feel wet, and before she could make sense of any of it, she was sitting in a puddle of water.

"The baby was crying, and the two of them were sitting there, at the mercy of this thing, waiting for the terror to end."

Everyone looked at me, and I kept talking.

"Finally, when it seemed like everything had calmed down, a feeling of relief came over her. She sat there thinking to herself, *finally. This is all over. We're safe. We're alive.* But when she climbed up from the storm cellar, do you know what she found?"

All eyes were on me.

"Nothing. Just *nothing.* She stood there where her house used to be. But there was no house. No fence. No couch. No nursery. No bed. Nothing. The storm took it all."

The waiter appeared and began setting down coffee cups, and my mimosa.

"Six months ago, I thought this was over," I said. "And now I'm standing where my house used to be and there's... nothing."

I looked down at the mimosa in front of me.

"Are you ladies ready to order?" the waiter asked.

"I think we need a minute," MJ said.

After he walked away, she looked my direction, reaching across the table to set her hand on top of mine.

"I think you're in a good place."

I stared at her blankly.

"*Seriously.* I think you're in the best place that I've seen you so far. I'm proud of you."

I couldn't have been more confused. I must not have been making myself clear. Perhaps I was being too metaphorical and should actually tell her about how last night, I had driven to David's house, and sat on his doorstep for a good 20 minutes before I realized that any minute he could come home with his four-year-old—or another woman for all I knew—and how the only thing that made me get in my car and drive home was thinking about how awkward that would be, to explain to one of his children who on earth I was.

I thought about telling her how I was waking up in the middle of the night, just about every night. Or about how I kept taking entire bottles of wine and pouring them into my Yeti cup, drinking them with a straw. Before I could say anything, MJ broke my train of thought.

"Do you remember when you first told me you were filing for divorce?"

I thought about it for a moment and shook my head. Everything had been such a blur after the separation.

"You were rock solid on the phone."

"I was?"

"Yes. You were just so stoic. I remember thinking: she's not being honest with herself. I mean, she's such a warrior woman. So strong. Holding things together, like a champion. But I just kept waiting for the moment when you would be a *human*, you know? I've been waiting for *you* to show up."

MJ set down her coffee cup.

"Is this me?"

"Is it?" She prompted. "I want you to let yourself feel this, Ally. Don't push it away. Don't try to pretend it's not happening. Let yourself feel it all the way. If you don't, it's going to keep coming back over and over again. It will keep trying to get your attention."

"It might kill me."

"What's going to kill you is holding onto it forever. It will be a slow and terrible death."

I thought about the past seven days. Slow and terrible death. Yes, that sounded about right.

"I never should have gotten myself into this mess with David," I said.

"I disagree," MJ said. "I don't think you could have done any of this without him. You needed David."

That actually sounded true to me.

"This is the most you I've ever seen you," MJ told me, and the rest of the women in the group nodded.

"You mean this disaster of a girl?" I laughed.

"Yes, *this* disaster of a girl. We love this disaster of a girl."

I thought about that for a minute. This girl was fragile and messy and so much less impressive than the girl I had been pretending to be. But for all her faults, she was true. She was herself.

The waiter came, and we each ordered breakfast and the pace of my breathing returned to normal. I wiped the mascara from under my eyes and Tracie kept her hand on my back for just a little bit longer. When we were all settled again, MJ caught my eye.

Welcome home," she whispered, smiling.

"To being a disaster!" Emily lifted her coffee cup.

"To being a disaster!" said Tracie—she and Lindsley lifting theirs, too. Our glasses oh-so-gently clinked together.

---

That night I sat at my house, alone. Deep in the quiet. This idea of coming home MJ was talking about—it sounded nice earlier, but now that I was here, in my home, I realized what a terrible idea this was. What a truly horrible idea. Because I did not want to be here, in my home. It did not feel good. What was I thinking?

I thought about turning on the TV, but instead I went to the fridge and found one of the last bottles of wine in the house. I counted in my head. Ten bottles had arrived at the beginning of the week. Two bottles were left, one in the fridge, one in the pantry. I rustled through the kitchen drawers, searching for one of my wine keys. I screwed the key into the cork and tried to leverage the bottle open. But the hook kept slipping from the edge of the bottle. I couldn't get it to catch enough to get the cork out.

"Damnit!" I screamed into the silence of the house. My voice echoed.

Slamming the wine key on the counter, I flung open the refrigerator door and put the bottle back inside. I went to the pantry and found the bottle of red that was there. Malbec. Not my favorite. Whatever. I screwed the key into the cork, leveraged, pulled, and the cork came out.

I poured the entire bottle into my Yeti cup and went back to sit on the couch.

From my perch there, I looked around the living room. I looked at the back door, the way the curtains had been tousled from the last person who had come through to see the place. There had been 20 showings in three weeks, and not one viable offer.

I picked up my phone to call David, but instead, I called my realtor.

"Ally!" he said when he answered the phone. "I was just about to call you."

"Hey Allen, calling to check in. Any news on the house?"

"It's the strangest thing. I can't figure it out. Your place should be selling. We should be getting dozens of offers. And we're just... not."

*Great, ok,* I thought to myself. *Isn't that just my luck.*

"What can I do Allen?"

"Unfortunately, I don't think there's anything you can do. At this point, it's just a waiting game."

I was so tired of waiting. I had been waiting for the past five years of my life. Waiting for things to change, waiting for them to be different, waiting for some kind of sign or some kind of instruction about how to get out of this mess I had gotten myself into. I considered telling him that I was good at a lot of things—give me a job and I'll get good at it—as long as that job *wasn't* waiting. I'm truly terrible at waiting. But then I realized all of that would be a very strange thing to tell your realtor.

"Thanks for your help. Will you keep me posted?"

"Of course. Take care."

We hung up the phone.

I considered texting David. I considered driving over to his house, again, but by now the wine I was drinking through a straw was starting to kick in.

Instead, I sent a text to Sarah. *I'm in the dark place. Not totally sober and thinking of driving to David's house. Can you help?*

Sitting there on my couch and clearly emotionally unstable is when the thought occurred to me: my house could be cursed. *Yes, it's probably cursed,* I thought to myself. It's cursed. That's why it wasn't selling.

That's also when I remembered a box of things I had been wanting to burn sitting in my trunk out in the car. My wedding quilt. Our marriage certificate. Checkbooks with my old last name. I thought maybe building a bonfire would be a good way to clear out the evil spirits.

To be honest, I had no idea how to build a fire, but what better time to build a fire for the first time than after you've had nearly an entire bottle of wine to yourself, am I right?

So I walked out to my car, barefoot, and collected the small box. When I looked up from the trunk, someone was standing on my front porch. It was Sarah—in all her flaming red-haired glory.

"What can I do, bunny?"

"Help me light a fire?"

We found a lighter in one of the kitchen drawers and grabbed some old Trader Joe's bags from under the kitchen sink. We walked out onto the back deck where the fire pit was, and I rustled through the pile of wood that had been sitting back there for months at least, if not a year— soaking wet.

"Can't see why this won't work," I said.

I ripped apart grocery bags into tiny pieces and threw them into the pit. Sarah looked at me and followed suit. The two of us stood there together, for several minutes, ripping bags and silently agreeing not to talk about how irrational this was, how totally ridiculous. I picked up two pieces of wood and piled them on top of the ripped bags.

"I don't know what I'm doing." I said, staring at the pit.

"I think maybe you do."

I held the lighter to the paper and waited for it to catch a flame. I had to do this several times, and Sarah kept ripping more and more and more paper, until the fire burned all the way through the wet part of the wood, so it could hold a flame. Finally we had a modest little fire going. We stood there, the two of us, staring at the way it burned.

"What now?" Sarah asked.

"I'm not sure yet."

As the fire burned, I thought about something I had read so many times in my life, but that hadn't come to my memory in years. *Blessed are the pure in heart, for they will see God*. It's from a passage called The Beatitudes, from the book of Matthew in the Bible.

The fire burned hot, and I burned hot with it.

I thought about what a pastor friend had told me about the word pure. In Greek, apparently the word is kataros—which is where we get the word cauterize—which literally means to *burn the flesh* of a wound, so it doesn't get infected. I thought about what MJ had said earlier about how this wasn't going to get better unless I let it hurt all the way.

Hurt all the way? Really? Couldn't I just let it hurt a little bit?

And by the way, why was it that the *burning* of a thing, this total undoing of something, could also be purifying? Why did *that* have to be the way we get to see God? I thought of Jesus, that day in the Garden of Gethsemane. *Take this cup from me,* he begged. It was all making so much sense now.

*Not my will but yours be done.*

I began throwing things into the fire, one by one. I took our wedding quilt and ripped it into shreds, at first angrily, throwing one piece in at a time and thinking about all the ways I had been betrayed and hurt, all the ways I had been tricked and lied to and pushed around and left behind and how I had kept coming back for more, over and over again.

Then, I did it with a little more softness—thinking about all the ways I had lied, and had pretended, and how I said yes when I meant no and how I had yelled and raised my voice and done my own fair share of leaving.

I watched how each thing I tossed into the flames would feed the heat of the fire.

Tears and makeup streaked down my face, and the fire blazed, and I stood there, barefoot and crying. I held up the little lace bolero I had worn on my wedding day. I held it to my face, wondering if I could still smell the perfume I had worn that day. I thought about the woman I had been back then, that day, the day I walked down that glowing aisle. I wondered if I could ever forgive her for what she had done to me.

I dropped that little bolero into the fire and let it burn, and let out a loud, guttural "huh" the way Sarah had me do in the yoga studio that day. It rang out over the neighborhood. The fire blazed on.

Finally, lastly, I held up my marriage certificate. I ran my finger over the writing on it, the writing that looked like my writing, but that also seemed like this distant and far-away person's writing, someone I had never met. I stared at it, in the glow of the firelight, and thought about how very final this made everything. This was over. I'd come up from the storm cellar and everything was gone. All that I had built.

I dropped the certificate in the fire and watched it burn.

Sarah looked at me.

"I'm proud of you," she said.

I put one hand on my belly and the other hand on my heart and Sarah did the same. We stood there together on my back deck, getting bitten a hundred times by mosquitoes, and I let the buzz of the wine wear off slowly and thought about how there are only really two choices in life—to hold on and be miserable, or to let go and surrender to the fire that is trying to purify us. This is it, I think. Love. Being in your life with your whole heart.

"I feel it all now, Sarah," I told her.

"Isn't it spectacular?" she said.

---

When I came back in the house, it was still quiet, but it felt different this time. A little more bearable. Sarah said her goodbyes and I thought of going to bed, but the idea of walking up to that room—*our* room— alone again was still too much. I had trudged up to that room alone so many times. Even when we were married, I had been alone in that room. I couldn't do it anymore.

Instead, I googled: *what to do if your house is cursed.*

I found an article that seemed as credible as an article about clearing evil spirits from your house can be. The first suggestion was to burn sage. I had heard of this before, and thought of doing it a few times, but I didn't have any sage on hand, and even though I was feeling more or less sober again, I didn't think it was probably a good idea for me to drive. So I kept reading.

The other option she gave was to ring a bell. Apparently the noise of the bell was supposed to break up stagnant energy. But, of course, I also didn't have a bell.

If you didn't have a bell, the author said, your last option was to walk through the space and do something that would make a bunch of noise. You could yell, or use a musical instrument, or you could bang pots and pans together.

*Pots and pans.* Hmm. I put my phone down and went barging into the kitchen, rustling through the cupboards. I pulled out two pots that seemed like they might make some good noise and I held them in my hands and just went for it.

I held those pots up in the corners of the living room and walked through each of the three bathrooms, in case the negative energy was hiding there, and walked out onto the back porch again, where the fire was hardly even glimmering anymore, and through each of the bedrooms. I just kept banging them together and making as much noise as I possibly could.

"Take that, evil spirits!" I said, banging those pots and pans together. "And that! And that!"

Then, as I walked back through the threshold of my house, I remembered how in the Old Testament, the Israelites would rub oil on the doorposts to bless a place. So I ran upstairs looking for a book of blessings I have by John O'Donohue—and found one for a new house. Then it was back to the kitchen to find some olive oil.

I rummaged through the pantry, but all I could find was a blend of cooking oils—coconut and grape seed oil.

"That should work, right?" I said out loud.

I couldn't see why not. I poured a little into my left hand and started making my way through the house, rubbing cooking oil on each of the doorways. Closets. Bathrooms. Bedrooms. Front door. Back door. Every single doorway got some oil.

"May this be a safe place, where you can be as you are, without any need of mask..." I read from the blessing.

When it was over, I sat on my couch, and felt strangely satisfied. I also felt totally insane. But doing something–even something a little crazy—helped me feel like I could go to sleep.

I walked up to my room. I felt bigger than I had before, a little older, and a little younger, too. I felt a little stronger and also more fragile. I stood at the door of my bedroom and stared inside. *May this be a safe place,* I whispered to myself, *where you can be as you are, without any need of mask.* Then, I walked through the door, and fell backwards onto the bed.

I lie there thinking about how I should get up and wash my face and brush my teeth and maybe put on some pajamas, but instead I listened to my own breath. In and out, in and out. I closed my eyes.

When I did that, I saw David's face first. We were sitting on the back porch of that little condo in Seaside, and the sun was setting, and the light was soft. Golden hour.

I thought about how innocent the two of us looked in that moment. I thought about what he said to me later that evening, about being a mess, and what he said to me that day at the juice bar—about how JD was doing the best he could. It was starting to make sense to me now. Most of us, most of the time, are doing the best we can.

It's not always ideal. But it is always our offering.

I thought about the morning I had gone down to the water, alone, and how I had let myself float in the ocean. I thought about what it felt like to give way to this thing that was more powerful than I was, about how good it felt to let go. I thought about how soft water was, how forgiving. What an amazing force the ocean was. Soft and strong. I wanted to be more like her.

In my mind's eye, I put my hand on David's chest and looked directly into his eyes. When I did that, a wave of sadness came over me. No anger. No desperation. Just sadness, because I missed him and I was grateful for him and I loved him. And because it was time to let go.

"I'm sorry, David," I whispered into the darkness. "I'm so sorry."

I thought about how much pain we cause people when we try to make them who we need them to be instead of letting them be who they are; how much pain most of us are suffering that no one will ever know.

Then, suddenly, without warning, it wasn't David standing in front of me anymore. It was JD. He seemed so much smaller than I had remembered him. Softer. Less intimidating. My hand was on his chest and I could feel his heart beating, and there, in that space, I softened to him. Like cement cracking, an ice cube melting in your water glass. It hurt. It hurt like hell. But I let it hurt all the way.

Between sobs, I found myself speaking words to JD that I never thought I would—and that I may not have been able to speak if I hadn't spoken them to David first. Such a mercy.

"I'm sorry, JD," I whispered. "I'm so sorry."

My whole body shook as I said the words, and I thought about Sarah. *Trembling is how we know we are in a relationship.* With that, I let it all go.

I cried and cried and cried. I felt all of it. Rode the wave of it. Let it crash over the top of my head. And when there were no more tears, I fell asleep. For the first time in over a week, I didn't wake up in the middle of the night.

The next morning, before I was even out of bed, I got a notification on my phone about another showing on my house that day. Then, before noon, three more showings. By 2:00 p.m., two more showings. I thought about texting my agent to tell him we were going to get an offer on the house—I could feel it—but before I could send the message, he texted me. *We've got an offer.*

When I think now about what it takes to find our way home, I wonder if letting go is the only way to do it. There is no formula, that's what I'm finding. Even our best and most beautiful attempts to get there are vein attempts. Our messiest, stupidest, most irreverent attempts might show us the thing we wanted most had always been with us. All this time.

It's taken me a long time to figure out who I've been all along.

More and more lately I'm believing I can trust this wave that seems to want to crash its way over my head. As terrible as it seems, it seems to me it is actually a wave of great mercy. My destruction is also my rebuilding. This ocean of grief is actually an ocean of love. It's so thick. It's soft and forgiving. It's everywhere.

It's almost like I am swimming.

# CHAPTER 14
# SWIMMING IN LOVE

---

*"You are a fighter. It is all you have ever known.*
*Drop the gloves.*
*Shake it out.*
*Love is yours."*

**—Jennifer Wyman**

Love is the hardest thing we will ever do and also the easiest. It is the most counter-intuitive thing to do and also the most natural. We were put here to love. We are born to love. It's so hard and so easy.

I'm convinced the thing that makes love the hardest is the letting go. Letting go of the way we thought things would go. Letting them be exactly as they are. Letting people make their own choices. Letting them walk away. Letting the outcome be what the outcome wants to be. We are not entitled to outcomes. We are only entitled to our effort. We can either be in love or be in control. Not both.

I'm learning to stay in love.

It is not without its challenges—staying in love—but the more I do it, the more I find myself feeling like no matter what happens, I am ok. I am secured to the earth with the force of lightning. I am supported and carried. I fall, but I do not shatter into a million pieces. I'm attacked, or lied about, or blamed, or pushed, but I am *indestructible*. I am a force to be reckoned with. Nothing can stop me.

It's not exactly what you think. It's not such a big production. It's the opposite of what you'd imagine. It's the opposite of what I always imagined it meant to be the kind of woman who was strong and confident and standing in her power—like Robi.

Small is big. You go down to go up. Soft is strong.

---

David did eventually call. We drove across town and met for breakfast one morning, and he told me he was sorry he did that disappearing act. He apologized a thousand times and told me he felt like a real jerk, but that he was dealing with some stuff, trying to stay with himself, trying to keep breathing. And because of everything that had happened, because of everything I know now, I told him I wasn't angry. In fact, I thanked him for telling me the truth.

"I was scared," he told me.

"Me too," I said.

We talked a bit more about our relationship and "making this work" and how we would move forward from here. But he kept saying he was wrapped up with this fear and dread, and he wasn't sure how he was going to find his way out. It was too much for him right now.

I wished I could do something. I wished I could reach out and touch him and help him see himself the way I saw him. Soft and strong. The way he looked at golden hour. But the truth was I was still figuring all of this out for myself. The most loving thing we can ever do for anyone is let them have their process.

I thought about fighting for this, fighting for him, fighting to make it work. Part of me still felt like that might be the most loving thing. But then I kept remembering how terrible it feels to be in control and how good it feels to stay in love. Surrender.

So I stayed with myself in that moment. I stayed with my breath. I stayed in my body. Soft is strong.

I let go.

I left breakfast thinking about how strange love was, how it was different than I ever thought. How odd it was that I felt more love for this man than I had felt in a long time, and I was still walking away from him. Here we were, totally apart and totally together—held in love, carried in love, just so covered in love that we couldn't have found our way out, even if we had tried.

———————

I sent an email to Mikey. I think it was saying goodbye to David that made me do it, since there are many ways to say goodbye to a person and this good, clean, honest goodbye to David made me realized how terrible my goodbye with Mikey had been. I wanted to see if I could get a better goodbye, if goodbye was still necessary. If it wasn't too late.

I had already reached out on Facebook once or twice and not heard back. So this time I sent an email.

The subject line read: *My offering*.

In the body of the email, I told him I was sorry. I said there was no way I could make up for what I had done, but that I was attaching a copy of a manuscript I had written—which was about what it meant to stay in love. I thanked him for loving me, and told him I loved him, and I said it would be great to hear from him sometime. Then I signed it.

*Love always, Ally.*

I walked to the yoga studio to meet Sarah.

It was winter again, and I had moved from my old house to a new, much smaller one—an apartment, actually. I had to get rid of over half of what I owned to make it all fit, but it was safe and warm and I was making it mine. It was also walking distance to the yoga studio.

I did my fair share of resisting this—the shifting of seasons. Somehow going back to the cold temperatures after all the softening, all the warming, sounded like the *worst* possible thing that could happen. I wanted it to last as long as possible, the softer part of grace. I didn't want to endure the unendurable anymore. I wanted to float in the ocean.

As it turns out, no matter how hard you try to resist change, it doesn't stop it from happening.

I headed back to the bathroom to change.

A few weeks earlier I had been at my parent's house. There were pictures hanging on the wall in the room where I was staying, pictures of me at 5 and 15 and 10. At certain moments, it was almost like I could reach out and touch that old version of myself. She was so close—that girl I had always been.

In one, I was 6 years old, sitting on the front porch swing with my big brother. I had my arms thrown around him in the biggest hug. My cheeks were naturally flushed, and my eyes were bright and blue, and I was smiling so big you could see my teeth.

In another, I was in a pink jumpsuit and holding a bright yellow daisy, nose pressed to the flower and just taking it all in.

I was so happy then. I can't help but think how natural it is for us to be happy, how easy it is to be happy when you are in love, when you are who you've been all along.

"You ready?" Sarah popped her head in the bathroom where I was changing.

"Yes, almost. Be there in two."

I pulled my shirt over my head and turned to walk out the door, but as I did, I caught a glimpse of myself in the mirror. I paused and looked, tilting my head. My tousled hair and flushed cheeks, the natural color of my lips without any lipstick. I stood there, staring for a minute at that face looking back at me.

I smiled, ever-so-slightly. *There she was.*

---

Sarah and I met in the extra studio where we always did our lessons. She had me set up my mat next to the wall, and then lay on my back, and put my feet up flat on the wall, so my legs were at right angle. She dictated instructions and I followed them.

"Push your feet into the wall," she explained, and I did.

"Can you feel that in your lower back?"

I nodded.

"How's David?" she asked, sliding her hand under my back to make a small adjustment. She always had this way of knowing things—knowing the right questions to ask, knowing just when to push and when to back off, knowing what exactly you or your body needed before even you knew you needed it.

"I haven't talked to him since our breakfast last month."

"And?" Sarah kept her hand at my back, working her way up slowly, until I could feel a release of pressure travel up my spine. I closed my eyes and reminded myself to just let it happen.

"And what?"

"How are you feeling?"

"Different on different days. One day I'm totally fine, the next day I'm in pieces. One day I feel like this is how it is supposed to be, and the next day I feel like we really missed it."

"Sounds about right."

She motioned to me to sit up, so I did. I sat criss-cross applesauce and she stood behind me, legs pressed firmly into my back for leverage, putting pressure on my shoulders with her hands. I breathed a sigh of relief. My shoulder was feeling better these days than it had felt in years.

"Have I ever told you about the last time I saw my ex?" she asked.

"I don't think so."

"We were sitting on his bed," she told me, "and we were playing this game we would always play, where I would name something and he would tell me it was cool or not. I'd be like, '*lions*,' and he would reply, '*not as cool as lionesses*.' I would say, '*lion tamers*' and he'd reply, '*respectable...*'"

She smiled at the memory, her whole face softening.

"At one point, Ally, I started to get angry. Because I could feel him pulling away from me. My eyes filled with tears. And without looking at him, I whispered, *I know you love me*."

I looked at her and she kept talking.

"A few minutes later, Ally, I looked back, and his eyes were full of tears too. And I *knew*. I just knew he loved me. I didn't need him to prove it. He always had. He always will. We haven't spoken in two years."

We sat in silence for a minute.

"I do not like that story, Sarah."

She laughed. "What don't you like about it?"

"I want a *love story*, you know?"

"You mean you want to get married and stay married forever?"

"Kind of!"

"I think you will."

"Sarah, that doesn't make any sense. I mean, you told me yoga would give me more love, less fear and more of what I want in my life. What am I doing wrong? Why isn't it working?"

"Let me get this straight," Sarah said. You've been divorced for how long?"

"A year."

"So in the past year, you've left a relationship where your entire life and business and friend circle were intertwined with this person—because it was toxic for you. You've sold your house. Moved. Sold your car. Changed your last name. Started a business. Fallen in love. Said goodbye to *that* man because you knew he could not give you what you needed."

I nodded. It did sound like quite the story when she laid it all out like that.

"It sounds like it's working, bunny. Love is working. You are doing it. Love is happening. Be patient."

I let Sarah move me from one position to another and, as she did, I wondered if she was right. If love was working, if it was already happening, and if I knew it didn't need any help, what would I do instead?

When I left Sarah, I went home and stood at the front door of this new apartment, thinking about all of the ideas I had for how to make it mine. My little space, something I could have some pride about. I picked up the phone and called a person who I thought might know me better than just about anyone. My sister.

"Hi," I said as soon as I heard her voice. "Can you fly to Nashville and help me with something?"

---

Sometimes we have to learn the same thing a thousand times before we really get it. We have to travel around the same block, looking at those same landmarks, dozens and dozens of times, before it all starts to make sense. It's like a labyrinth—no straight line to the center, just turn after turn, twist after twist, lesson after lesson, again and again. Sometimes closer, sometimes further away. The lesson goes deeper each time. We never run out of chances.

I left for the airport and stopped on the way at my favorite coffee shop to grab something warm to drink. While I stood in line, I felt a hand on my shoulder. I turned around to see my friend Thad.

"Thad! Where have you been?"

"California" he said, smiling. He seemed different to me. Softer.

"What were you doing in California?"

He told me the story of how he had met a girl, and how there was something different about her, and how he'd been flying to California to spend time with her. I had known Thad for awhile now, and I had never seen him act like this about a girl.

"Thad, could this girl be *the* girl?"

"You know, at 40 years old, I've learned not to make too many assumptions about that kind of stuff," he told me. "But I pray the same prayer for her that I pray for all of my friends."

"What's that?"

"It goes like this. May you grow everyday in the knowledge of God's love for you. May that knowledge bring you great healing. And through that healing, may you become all you were intended to be."

I took a deep breath. I loved that.

Just then, Thad's name was called and he went up to the counter to get his coffee. We hugged, and he turned to leave.

I thought about the prayer he prayed and about how I wanted to know that kind of love, the ever-expanding kind of love, the healing kind of love, the always-there kind of love. The kind of love that was so thick you could swim in it.

"Hey Thad," I said. He looked at me. "Can I be your friend?"

I laughed, because what I had *meant* to say was, *Can I be one of the friends you pray that prayer for?* But Thad didn't seem phased. He laughed a little, too, and before he turned again to leave, he smiled.

"You *are* my friend," he said, waving and walking out the door.

I kept waiting for my coffee, spinning and shining and wondering, quietly, why it is we are grasping at so many things we already have.

———————

I drove to pick my sister up the from the airport, and we spent the next three days together, building my new space from scratch—this small and simple, ordinary, down-to-earth space. It wasn't big or flashy. It wasn't earth-shattering. But it was mine, and I was starting to think I might actually love it.

I unpacked the remaining boxes and learned to install my washer and dryer, and my sister and I laughed at our inability to operate a power drill. We drank wine and watched Gilmore Girls and listened to country top 40. When we were all done, we flopped onto the couch and looked around.

"Not half bad," my sister said, smiling.

I looked at her.

"Hey, I'd say it's even better than that!"

I got up and walked to the kitchen, where I grabbed the bottle of wine. When I came back to sit on the couch, that's when I saw it. The thing I never expected to see, the very thing I had wanted to see for so long. My jaw fell open, and I turned the computer toward my sister.

"Look," I said.

"Mikey…"

The email said: *I forgive you, Ally. And I love you, too. Next time you're in Portland, come meet my wife and my son. Maybe we can all have brunch.* ☺

We looked around the apartment at what we had done, and I thought about what I had not done—which was to force anything. I hadn't done anything more than tell the truth. I let the idea of love and of healing wash all the way over me. It was so simple and so revolutionary, this tiny little bit of love unfolding.

Like Sarah said, it was happening.

My sister and I said goodnight, and I went into my bedroom. When I got in there, I saw a box of books I'd forgotten to unpack, so I lowered myself to the floor and lifted the flap slowly, pulling books out, one by one. I placed them each carefully on my new bookshelf. When I reached into the box to grab the final one, something fluttered out of one of them. A small piece of white paper.

When I saw what it was, I nearly fainted.

At the top of the page, in bold letters, was printed the name *David Garrison*. Then, handwritten in black ink across the paper, the note said, simply: *Just a note to remind you how remarkable you are. Truly, one of the most beautiful people I've ever met. Love you. Always.*

The tears started to come, and then the laughter, quiet laugher, because this was funny, actually. Just so funny. I cried, and I giggled at how stupid it was, really, thinking we ever lose anything we've always had. To think that we can ever be anything but held completely in love. I shook with joy. I shook with grief. I laid all the way down on the ground, on my back, holding that tiny piece of white paper to my chest, right to my heart.

And here she was—in this new place that wasn't yet familiar, but that was all hers—the same little girl who sat on the porch swing with her arms thrown around her big brother. Here was the girl with the yellow tulip in her hands, gently smiling.

Here she was.

She'd been here all along.

# AFTERWARD
# SOFT IS STRONG

---

*For one human being to love another: that is perhaps the most difficult of all our tasks, the ultimate, the last test and proof, the work for which all other work is but preparation.*
**—Rainer Maria Rilke**

'm writing this book at the ocean because I needed to be here. It is actually November now, not just the drizzly November of my soul anymore. It is election month, and I have to say, I have never felt more in my life like knocking people's hats off.

Last night I went to dinner in a small town called Seaside. I sat at the bar counter by myself because this is what you do when you're single and traveling alone. Shortly after I sat down, a young man walked up to me and introduced himself. His name was Todd. He was handsome and tall, and he offered to buy me a second glass of wine. I accepted. For thirty minutes we did the thing you do—talking about the weather and sports and business and politics. Then he asked me what I was doing here, at the ocean.

"I'm writing a book," I said.

"What's your book about?"

"It's about love."

Right then, something was happening on the TV behind the counters. It was Donald Trump. It is just Trump and Hillary left now, and we're waiting to see who will be the one. I've been thinking for months how certain I am it will be Hillary—how it *has* to be Hillary—because I cannot imagine the alternative. And I also have to keep reminding myself that nothing has to be *anything*.

Nothing is guaranteed. We are never entitled to our outcomes. Only to our efforts.

Todd and I really got into it when we started talking about Trump. He was a big Trump guy, and I was not a big Trump girl, and he had all of his reasons and I had all of mine. We had a decent conversation about it, to be honest. Nothing too heated or mean. But at the end of everything, Todd said something to me that I felt like proved my whole point, that really summed up this entire book.

"Can I be honest with you?" he asked.

I nodded.

Then he went on, and I nearly regretted giving him permission to be honest—since his idea of telling the truth was to talk about me.

"I think your book idea sucks," he said.

My jaw dropped. I sat there for a minute, trying to figure out how you are supposed to respond to something like that from a perfect stranger, and how on earth he thought a comment like that was going to get him where he was trying to go. Seeing my shock, he tried to defend himself.

"It's a compliment," he kept saying. "You're smart. You seem like you have good things to say. Why waste your words on a book about love?"

There were so many things I wanted to say to him in that moment, so many things I wanted to do. Most of it involved a kind of kicking motion and all kinds of foul language. But you know what? I didn't say anything. I realized what this was, this feeling I felt. I didn't want to be here. I felt like a Christmas ornament.

And as soon as that feeling came over me, I dropped my defenses. I didn't want to kick him anymore. I wanted to cup his face in my hands, like he was 9 years old. I wanted to tell him I was sorry. I wanted to ask him what he was doing there, in a bar, buying a pretty girl a drink, if love didn't matter. I wanted to tell him he seemed sad and lonely.

And then I wanted to whisper to him, really softly, but oh-so-firmly—that he deserved it. All of it. Everything he ever wanted.

Instead, I said nothing. I paid my tab, and I took my things, and I walked home alone, with my feet in the sand, listening to the ocean. In and out, in and out. She's so beautiful, don't you think?

---

Last night, I had this dream. David and I were at dinner together. He told me he knew he had hurt me, had left me, and how it kept him up at night—that idea of having broken my heart.

I looked across the table and just said, "It is so amazing, David. The whole thing. Nothing is broken. You are remarkable."

"I'm no better than your ex-husband," he said.

I watched him hang his head when he said that. I felt like I knew what he was thinking because I've thought it so many hundreds of times myself—about being such a failure, such a terrible failure. I felt it with him. Love teaches us to feel everything.

When I opened my mouth to speak again, I reached my hand across the table. I said, "me neither, David. Neither are any of us."

I meant it. I really did.

The strangest feeling came over me that moment, something so perfectly unexpected. Do you know what it was? It was *hope*. I felt strangely hopeful for all of us. I kept thinking about how *amazing* it is that we're all just thrown into this life without a handbook, and how we are fumbling along, making our way, doing our best.

Most of us don't even really change over the years. Not that much anyway. But some of us, a few of us, we show up and we breathe and we get the littlest bit better at grace. Enduring the unendurable. Making space for blessings as they come. And eventually we are soft but also strong. When someone comes at us, we don't cut them. When we fall, we do not shatter into a million pieces.

What a big, beautiful, spectacular thing we're doing—being in our bodies. Being in love.

David and I both sat there in the silence for the longest time. I wanted to say so much more. There was *so much more* I wanted to say— about the light I saw in him and how incredible I thought he was. *What a grace.* I wanted to say. *What a grace it has been to hurt this way with you, to sit with you in the darkness of our pain. What a grace it has been to be here together, even if just for a minute. Thank God. Love is having its way with us.*

But I think, somewhere deep down, he already knew.

———————

I woke from that dream in a soft, warm place. Light was barely streaming in the windows. I walked to the back porch, barefoot and in my pajamas, and down to the beach. And right there, in front of the ocean, I did yoga, alone. I didn't do it perfectly. Couldn't remember all the moves.

But I did it anyway, and felt so free. I felt like a dancer on a stage, for an audience of only one.

Sometimes the hardest person to have grace for is yourself, you know? For being imperfect, for not always getting it right, for learning as we go, for fumbling, for loving hard and fast and long. For forgetting to love, for raising our voices, for not raising our voices when we needed to most. For having second thoughts, for jumping into things, for jumping out of things, for moving on, for getting hung up and held back, for giving something a try, for not feeling ready to give it a try.

But grace. Grace like a flood. If we can let it in, it restores us, returns us to ourselves, no matter how far we've gotten. It's all right in front of us. All of it. Everything we ever wanted.

As I stood by the ocean, doing the moves in the only way I knew how, I started to feel like maybe everything was going to be ok. No matter what came next. And the more I did it—the yoga, the breathing, the standing there all radiant and free in front of the ocean—the more I started to feel it. I was pretty sure it was happiness.

I giggled. Like Sarah.

And I can't be certain, but I think the ocean was singing to me as I danced in front of her. *Shhhhhh, shhhhhh,* she kept whispering. I felt so big, and so small. I felt like such a miracle.

It's taken me a long time to figure out who I have been all along.

# Morgan James
# Speakers Group

We connect Morgan James published
authors with live and online events
and audiences who will benefit
from their expertise.

Morgan James makes all of our titles available
through the Library for All Charity Organization.

www.LibraryForAll.org

CPSIA information can be obtained
at www.ICGtesting.com
Printed in the USA
BVHW07s2328021018
529120BV00003B/6/P

9 781683 509752